A SHORT HISTORY OF PERUGIA

M. GRAZIA NICO OTTAVIANI

S0-AXE-376

30

Pacini
Editore

Piccola
Biblioteca
Pacini

© Copyright 2010 by Pacini Editore S.p.A.

ISBN 978-88-6315-143-5

English translation
Lola Teale

INDEX

From the Etruscan and Roman City to the Medieval Commune

Over the centuries, the city of Perugia has been favoured by its geographical location, which overlooks the plain crossed by the river Tiber, and which stands on the axis linking the Adriatic Sea with the Thyrrhenian Sea. Furthermore the city, and especially its town centre, is situated in between two hills (Sole and Landone), which give it a unique appearance.

Many different theories abound for the origin of the city with numerous and apparently contradictory ancient sources: some are of the opinion that Perugia was founded by the Achaeans, descendants of the mythic Achaeus; in others' opinion the city was established by Euliste, the Etruscan founder of Bologna (Felsina). This latter opinion could relate the foundation of the city of Perugia with the Etruscan expansion in the Po Valley during the second half of the 6th century BC. Other sources link Perugia with the Umbri Sarsinati who, 'descending from the valley of the Savio and Mareccia to the northern area of the river Tiber, passed through western Umbria, settling in Perugia and in the area surrounding Lake Trasimeno from where they went to Chiusi'.

As to the geographical location, the city was situated in the area to the right of the river Tiber, traditionally an Etruscan area, but bordering with the zone inhabited by the Umbri who settled on the far side of the river. This river has always had 'in ancient times not only a role as division or border but also a role as means of commercial and cultural exchange between the populations settled along its banks'.

Thus Perugia has a dual origin, Etruscan and Umbrian, that makes it similar to another important city along the course of the Tiber, Todi (*Tuder*), an Etruscan town as substantiated by the remains of its necropolis, and with Umbrian origins as demonstrated by its local language. Furthermore these two cities were (and still are) linked together by the Via Amerina that, by connecting Orte, Amelia, Todi and Perugia, and then Chiusi, maintained the unity of the Etruscan and Umbrian areas. There were also other roads, besides the Via Amerina, that ran through the area of Perugia: on the one side it was connected to Cortona and Arezzo, and on the other with the Adriatic passing through Gubbio, another important Etruscan town. Thus, as A. Grohmann wrote, 'since the Etruscan period the history of Perugia and the fortune of the city has to be read in relation to the history of the environment where the main town in Umbria is situated, and to the important road network of the very same area, which sees Perugia almost at the centre of a junction between north and south, and between the east and the large Mediterranean area'. In conclusion, the town was part of the twelve confederate cities of Etruria, including Veio, Cerveteri, Tarquinia, Vulci, Volsini (Orvieto), Chiusi, Vetulonia, Volterra, Cortona, Arezzo, and Fiesole. This confederation administered not only treaties and alliances but also maintained a balance of power between the confederate cities. The necropolis with their funerary furnishings bear witness to the relationship and the influence coming from the nearby and powerful Chiusi. This is highlighted by the sarcophagus called of the *Sperandio* (named after the location of the discovery), which today is in the Archaeological Museum in Piazza Giordano Bruno. Its material and stylistic ornaments reveal that it came from Chiusi. On the two shorter sides, it shows two scenes of banqueting which is a traditional element in the archaic Chiusi reliefs, while on the front is depicted an extraordinary scene which has been interpreted in various different ways: the long cortege there represented, with male, female, child and animal figures (amongst which a donkey loaded with maybe a booty) might narrate the return from a battle, or from a military raid, or the transfer of a family into a new territory to be colonized, in this case the family of a Chiusi chieftain moving to Perugia in the period of the great migrations from Chiusi to the Tiber valley favoured by King Porsena in the 6th century. But this same scene might be interpreted also as the transfer of commanders from Perugia to territories beyond the Appennines after the colonization in the 6th century; or, as a last hypothesis, the protagonist of this relief might be an inhabitant of Perugia who was celebrating his triumph over the Umbrian people.

Whichever of the theories is correct, the most important element is the evidence of that remarkable vitality that Perugia has shown since the middle of the 6th century onwards, that is confirmed by many remains of remarkable importance, even written remains, as the bucchero cup with an Etruscan alphabet. This cup is linked to the later and more famous *Cippo Perugino* (dated to the 3rd and 2nd centuries BC, displayed in the Archaeological Museum) which appears as a block of travertine shaped like a parallelepiped, on whose front is to be found one of the longest Etruscan inscriptions known today. It referred to (although with still much uncertainty as to the interpretation) a contract between two families for the property of an area to become a burial ground.

The vitality and wealth of the city increased from the middle of the 5th century to the early 3rd century BC, as testified by the tombs dated to this period. These tombs with their rich funerary furnishings were of the upper classes, and no relevant evidences has been found to date for the lower social classes. The similarities between the furnishings, both as concerns the kind of objects and the materials used, is clear evidence of a very close-knit society, or at least as concerns its emerging upper class. In male tombs the furnishings included defensive armour such as helmets, greaves, fragments of shields, or offensive weapons such as bronze or iron lances, swords and curved broadswords. The Archaelogical Museum preserves matching remains such as a bronze sword (from Fontivegge) and the funerary furnishing from the Frontone necropolis. But the excavations in necropoleis have brought to light also female tomb furnishings of refined manufacture: earrings and gold rings, mirrors, bone ornaments, a small bronze box for jewellery (*cista*) with a siren on the cover.

Certainly, the 3rd century represents a period of disruption in the history of Etruria. Rome had already commenced a political policy detrimental in the first place to the southern Etruscan cities and later to the northern cities. The Etruscan front (of which Perugia was part together other cities united in the Italic army) suffered heavy defeats, amongst which the one in Sentino in 295 BC, and from then on came a 'definitive decline of the Etruscan power and the end of its long-lasting dream'. But Rome laid down conditions that were not particularly onerous, and did not suffocate the vitality of these towns; in the case of Perugia we assist in the 3rd century 'to an intense rural activity also testified to by the creation of new necropoleis halfway between the city and the countryside', such as the one of the Palazzone (in Ponte San Giovanni) which skirts the slope bordering on the river Tiber. There also was a change in the burial habits that probably reflects a 'social change'. The burial inside a sarcophagus, that allowed one or a maximum of two interments, became ever rarer and was substituted by the more practical cremation with ashes enclosed in funerary urns, which might also have gathered together all the members of a family clan. This custom became almost the norm in the 2nd and 1st centuries BC in Perugia and in other cities such as Chiusi and Volterra, and went hand in hand with the diffusion of funerary urns, mostly made of travertine but sometimes also of sandstone and terracotta, according to custom within the various territories of Etruria. At the end of the 3rd century BC, Perugia was again involved in an important battle, the war between Hannibal and Rome, whose army was defeated disastrously on Lake Trasimeno. The construction of the perhaps most prestigious monument of the Etruscan Perugia, the perimeter wall, dates to those years (end of the 3rd century and early 2nd century, or the middle of the 3rd century BC) and is still visible and well preserved in several tracts. It measured *in toto* about three kilometres surrounding the Acropolis, and thus the two hills (Landone and Sole), and their immediate vicinity; the unmistakable great parallelepiped blocks of travertine were (and still are) positioned in regular rows, and joined together without the use of cement ('*con maraviglioso artifitio senza calcina, congiunte insieme*') consistent with a typical construction technique of the time. The general impression is that it was not built piecemeal but rather designed and built in a relatively short period of time by teams working in converging directions. Also the cistern-well, called Etruscan or *di Sorbello* – named after the family who owned the palazzo from which it can be reached – would seem to date to the same period. This is situated under Piazza Piccinino, thus at the foot of the Acropolis, and its upper level was built with the same construction technique as that of the walls, to be specific with a lining of parallelepiped blocks of travertine. It supplied water to the city for a very long time, even up until recently.

Returning to the walls, an unequivocal stretch is that situated in Via della Cupa, as is the other in Via Cesare Battisti where the gate, called Etruscan Arch or Porta Pulchra or Arch of Augustus, is situated. This is the only original gate preserved and still with two towers of a trapezoidal shape and with an ornamental façade in its centre, with a Renaissance *loggetta* added in the 16th century. Two inscriptions had been added in the Roman period: *Augusta Perusia* (donated by Emperor Augustus) on the inferior arch, and *Colonia Vibia* at the base of the frieze (donated by Emperor Vibius Trebonianus Gallus who came from Perugia). Other gates of the ancient town (*vetus urbs*) even though no longer in their original form are: the Porta Trasimena, or arch of San Luca and the Porta Eburnea, or arch of the Mandorla both surmounted by a gothic medieval arch, and together with them the well-known Porta Marzia whose top was dismantled by Antonio da Sangallo the Younger in order to be positioned in the Rocca Paolina which was under construction around about the year 1540.

Between the end of the 2nd century BC and the beginning of the following century, Etruria appeared ever more 'immersed in the exploitation by rich landowners coming from a limited group of families', coupled with a dangerous 'alienation from the most important commercial activities in the Mediterranean area'. In 130 BC, the election of Perperna, probably from Perugia, as Consul, favoured the granting of Roman citizenship to a number of local people. This custom, which was extended and continued up until a complete Romanization, came about reinforced by the alliance of the Etruscans and Umbri with Rome in the *Bellum Sociale* (due to the agrarian law). After, Perugia was ruled by a government made up of four Roman officials (*quattuorvirato*) and Latin was adopted as official language, as is demonstrated by the burial inscriptions. But not long afterwards the city was, against its will, a protagonist of another dramatic event: the *Bellum Perusium*. The circumstances are fairly well-known: after Caesar's death and after the power struggle between Mark Anthony and Augustus, the former's brother, Lucius Anthony – who was elected consul in 41 BC in order to defend his brother's military positions, brother who still was in the Middle East with Cleopatra – took shelter in Perugia considering it a strong strategic military position. The above was narrated by Appianus and Cassius Dio, two Greek historiographers who were well informed of the events. Augustus promptly went there with haste and besieged Perugia, building around it a stockade and a ditch against which the numerous and continuous attempts to breakthrough by Lucius Anthony were to no avail. He, eventually, had no other alternative than to come to an agreement with Augustus, who raised the siege of the city promising to free the enemy soldiers (excluding the three hundred mortal enemies who were killed, but it maybe that the number was exaggerated). After the siege, Perugia was in a pitiful condition, 'the town centre had been almost totally destroyed by a fire, the most important families decimated, the political class practically inexistent', but had the advantage of a complete reconstruction by Augustus that gave it the title of Augusta, and he sustained its revival, entrusting it to some of the families of the gentry and to other important individuals who had become wealthy thanks to rapid and fortunate careers, who contributed to the revival even architectural of the town. Thus Perugia, during the imperial period, expanded outside the Etruscan walls, as testify the ruins of the amphitheatre (in the area of Palazzo della Penna today museum and exhibition area) and the mosaic, called of Sant'Elisbetta in the area of the Conca, representing Orpheus while enchanting many animals of very different species with the notes of his lyre. This clearly was a thermal complex which later was used as a place of Christian cult as some inscriptions here found 'of a probable sacred use' suggest.

After the fall of the Roman Empire and the upheaval that followed, another dramatic event, inevitably a war, brought Perugia to the foreground: in fact the city was involved in the war between the Goths and the Byzantines (the Gothic War) for the control of the peninsula.

Totila, King of the Goths and main protagonist, was ruthless towards the Umbrian towns especially against those situated along Via Flaminia and Via Tiberina, the two main roads which linked the Byzantine Rome and Ravenna. Both Gregory the Great in his *Dialogi* and Procopius of Caesarea (*Storia delle Guerre di Giustiniano*) give us some historical information about this 'almost impenetrable period in the history of Perugia'. We learn that at the time Perugia was besieged by the Goths, a long and gruelling siege that only ended in about 458, when Totila got the better of the valiant resistance of the inhabitants of Perugia supported by Bishop Ercolano, on whom fell the fierce revenge of the Gothic King who threw the dismembered body of the bishop from the city walls. After forty days that same dismembered corpse was disinterred and was found 'incorrupted and without any sign of mutilation', as narrates the *Passio*, the history of the life and martyrdom of the Saint written by Gregory the Great, shortly afterwards. Further this miracle of the exhumation and of the subsequent transfer of the saintly body to the church of San Pietro (firstly, later in the Cathedral) can be admired in the series of frescoes by Benedetto Bonfigli in the chapel of the Priori inside the Palazzo with the same name. During the years of siege, not only did the city suffer hardship but also the surrounding area. Totila destroyed the bridges across the Tiber and together with them also the town of Arna, once a Roman *municipium* then seat of the bishop, located strategically ten kilometres to the east of Perugia.

After Totila's defeat and death by the Byzantine general, Narses, (in 552, in the battle of Tagina near Gualdo Tadino), Perugia returned not without hindrance under the control of Byzantium, and this permitted a certain amount of recovery, which turned out to be very useful in the face of the fierce Lombard invasion. That of the Lombards is described by contemporaries as the most ferocious invasion of the entire Italic peninsula, and this is particularly true for Perugia. It put up a resistance with its Byzantine garrison, as did Gubbio, Todi, Amelia and Narni, all of them dangerously close to the Lombard Duchy of Spoleto, and inside the 'Byzantine corridor', a strip of land used also for linking Rome and Ravenna, this latter the capital city of the Exarchate ruled by Byzantium together with the Pentapolis (the coastal cities of the Marche region up to Osimo), Rome with its surrounding area, and part of Southern Italy. In order to break that link, but above all to join together the zones conquered, the Lombards attacked Perugia more than once conquering it twice, but were unable to keep it as the Byzantines had always been capable of recapturing it and controlled it for lengthy periods. The city was able to contain the might of the Lombards of Spoleto, as did Chiusi and Arezzo, thanks to an articulate defensive system which made the most of the morphological characteristics of the area (rivers, hills, woodlands and marshes) combining them with military defences strategically located along the minor roads and along the borders. Thus a vast area was created with the aforementioned characteristics, a Duchy of Perugia whose centre was Perugia itself and whose defensive positions were the Tiber, Lake Trasimeno and its marshes, the surrounding hills and furthermore the mountains to the north of the lake and to the south between the valley of the river Nestóre, and Orvieto. Thanks to these favourable circumstances, Perugia and the inland areas saw in the 7th century 'a slow but continuous economic upsurge' together with a political and administrative development entrusted, in the case of Perugia, to a *magister militum*, a type of Duke before his time, with military and civil power that tended to increase over time.

The situation changed with the arrival of the Franks called by Pope Stephen II in order to halt the Lombard expansion, as was the case of Aistulf who conquered Ravenna. When, in 755-756, Pepin the Short, Charlemagne's father, conquered the cities of the Exarchate and of the Pentapolis and gave them to the Pope as a gift, the Byzantine Duchy of Perugia fell to the same destiny. This is the beginning of a different historical age, one that saw Perugia and other Umbrian cities gravitating, not without challenges, in the area which was to become the Papal States.

In these years, both in Perugia and elsewhere, the key figure of the bishop came to the forefront. In some areas the bishop, in the period of the Germanic invasions, played the role of city defender, entrusted with administrative responsibility, besides that of bishop and head of the diocese. In Perugia, even though there is no clear evidence of a public authority run by the bishop before the communal period, although here the bishop was considered as 'the guarantor of the efficient functioning of the city, the interpreter of collective interests, the representative of the unity of the inhabitants and the unity between the city and its environs'. He was the point of reference for the social cohesion between the inhabitants – in short the social cohesion between all free men who considered themselves as such – who lived inside the city walls and formed a unique entity. Under the guidance of the bishop a group, an elite, was formed and made up of men (*boni homines*, initially without internal hierarchical distinction) who took up office in the name of the community, thus who acted for the common interest. Later on, from the 12th century, this was identified with the Commune, the revolutionary city institution, a new political feature inside the Empire which introduced important innovation: the establishment of a council of Consuls who, even though using 'Classic' terminology, represented the city in a revolutionary way, from an independent stance. The consular class appeared as an 'eminent part of the community' – both for social prestige and wealth – a group of inhabitants who served the city also with the inhabitants consent.

The social composition of the consular class was heterogeneous: there were not only the *milites* (the aristocratic mounted soldiers of proven ability) but also the members of the emerging merchant families and finally people of various professions, such as judges, doctors and notaries. The number of the members of the consular council varied over time from five to fifteen, this had led to the opinion that in the early period of the Commune this council was not a stable structure but created purposely to tackle urgent affairs (military operations, treaties, public order and administration). Then by the 1180s the appointment became yearly, and the number was fixed in fifteen members, normally three members from each district of the city, to whom was added the *Cameraio*, an official initially considered a member of the council as the others but given a specific responsibility, administration and control the Communal finances.

In 1186 Henry VI ratified, once and for all, this new institution with an act of foundation. This was a very important step, because Frederick I Barbarossa's son on officially endorsing in the city of Perugia the Consulate and the property of its surrounding countryside, which covered more or less the diocesan area, definitively confirmed 'that independence, that important role undertaken by the public authorities, that ample authority enjoyed and exercised for a long period of time' by including it once and for all in the Imperial civil code. A few years later, in 1198, Pope Innocent III endorsed the Consulate and approved the city regulations, taking it under his protection. This brought serious repercussions.

But at the same time the communal authority became a more institutionalized establishment, that meant a more streamlined and professional group of administrators: no longer the consular body, with a collegial and undefined structure, but a single 'individual in charge', an official *super partes* – both authoritative and professional – who became the symbol of the city, in one word the Podestà, initially a local inhabitant and later a foreigner, for a limited period alternating with the Consuls, and then from 1232 the sole official with executive, judicial and representative powers of the Commune. The turnover in the differing forms of government between the end of the 12th century and the early 13th century is a clear evidence of tensions inside the governing class, but the Commune had acquired its authority by being administered by a class of professionals, thanks to which Perugia exited from this period of institutional turnover strengthened and with the characteristics of a real administrative authority in comparison with the other towns in Umbria. As concerns the formation and the relationship with its *con-*

tado, the area outside the walls, Perugia is a model. Its *contado* was originated before the communal period with borders that more or less coincided with those of the dioceses. Thus, when considering Perugia, we can say it had not acquired them by conquest or expansionism as the Commune ever since the proto-communal period had controlled the dioceses. Over time Perugia carried out a programme to homogenize and to increase its *contado* in order to control better the border areas, going beyond, if necessary, the dioceses borders.

The increase in its *contado* was made through the agreements of submission (well-known as *Sommissioni*, a mutual agreement probably resulting from heavy pressures by the ruling city). This kind of agreement became ever more customary from 1180 to the early 13th century, and produced a real increase in the size of the *contado,* even though over time it did happen that the agreements were renegotiated. The lake and the *Chiugi* (the area between the lake and the Chiane known as the 'granary of Perugia'), Assisi, Città di Castello, Gubbio, Gualdo Tadino, Fossato and Nocera. The agreements of submission included also the noble families or the noble clans with whom Perugia created differing relationships during the period of maximum expansion, between the end of the 12th century and the 1360s and 1370s. There were a total of fifteen families, who boasted properties outside the diocese of Perugia, over which the Commune accepted only to have political control without having direct ownership of these properties. These aristocratic families (the Counts of Coccorano, the Marquis of Valiano, the Counts of Marsciano and others) were forced to become inhabitants of Perugia and to own a residence inside the perimeter walls, but they preserved their feuds, where they preferred living carrying on a lifestyle more appropriate to their social *status*.

Perugia and its People

The consular regime gave way to a Podestà during the first two decades of the 1200s. The choice of a Podestà as a sole official administrator (the first in Perugia is documented in 1195) answered, as mentioned in the previous chapter, the need to streamline and at the same time to improve professionally the public administration, but it was also a consequence of the inability of the Consulate to resolve the ever more frequent conflicts between *milites* and *pedites*, aristocracy and commoners. Initially the Podestà was chosen from amongst the *milites*, that same social class from where the consuls came. Later the Podestà was summoned from further afield but always from politically similar cities (in the case of Perugia, from Rome or Florence). The duties were always those which concerned 'the prosperity of the city', and thus render justice, collect taxes, represent the Commune, maintain public order, and administer the *contado*. In order to do this, the Podestà needed and brought with him a 'family' of judges, notaries, partners and guards. The Podestà and his 'family' enforced and conformed to a complex system of rules and regulations, composed of customs and laws issued by the Commune, these were the statutes, which during the 1200s and the 1300s were completely re-elaborated, unified and drafted. The earliest statute of Perugia, in existence, is in Latin and was written in 1279; the first text in an early Italian language (*volgare*) goes back to 1342 and was written in everyday language. The word 'people' had in this period a meaning completely different to that of the present day, it referred to all business people (artisans, shop-keepers and merchants). During the Middle Ages some businesses were organized in guilds with the aim to promote the production, control the market, and give assistance to their members. That said not all business activities were capable of creating a guild (the employees had always been excluded), nor did the guilds all have the same prestige – well-known is the distinction between major and minor guilds – but in general this corporative phenomenon affected all the Italian Communes, where the guilds came to have a relevant political role. A typical figure of the government of the guilds was the Capitano del Popolo, originally a true political leader, who collaborated with the Podestà, a professional official of the Commune, with similar responsibilities.

Perugia is the example of a city where the government of the people, the political expression for the most important guilds – the *popolo grasso* different from the *popolo minuto* made up of small artisans and employees in the manufacturing sector – had a long and prosperous existence. Documentary evidence of the government of the populace began in 1255 with the establishment of a Capitano del Popolo, who was a representative of the *popolo grasso*, in short merchants, money-lenders and members of the major guilds which in reality administered the political together with the economic power. Born from the guilds was the College of the Consuls of the Guilds which, established in 1266, became the pivot of the communal government up until the early 14th century. This body was made up of five members: two merchants, a money lender and by rotation two from the other guilds and collaborated with another important body, the Council of the People, established more or less in those same years. Without doubt the years that followed were the most favourable in the history of Perugia, characterized by a substantial harmony amongst the social classes and based on a non-violent lifestyle. This situation came to an end in the 1280s when this equilibrium deteriorated with the war against Foligno (1282-1283) which was the cause of financial difficulties and restrictive economic measures, and later in the 1290s it collapsed after a series of further administrative measures overturned the positive public image and the credibility of the Consuls of the Guilds. These measures were of a fiscal and financial nature (increasing direct taxation for all the population and the fiscal burden for the *contado*) and also touched immigration (limiting the relocation to the city). The immediate consequence of these measures was a general discontent in the lower classes of the city and the rural inhabitants who felt disadvantaged and especially swindled by the ruling oligarchy. The disintegration was inevitable, on the one side there was the *popolo grasso* who continued to lose influence, and on the other side there was the *popolo minuto* who no longer felt represented by the city government. Thus they reorganized themselves, no longer concerned by the detachment from the major guilds, and pushed for more influence in the city government. After several power struggles from both sides and a deterioration in the conflict due to a long-lasting famine, that from 1301 for three years starved the populace, especially the poor, the *popolo minuto* got the better of the situation and in

1302 imposed its will summoning Riccardo Frangipani from Rome to occupy the office of defender of the Commune (*defensor communis*). The first act of Frangipani was to condemn the Consuls of the Guilds in office during the previous December and January, with the consequent destruction of the authority and legitimacy of that body and thus compromising the political situation once and for all. The magistracy of the Consuls of the Guilds was abolished and substituted with the Priori of the Guilds, a political expression of the *popolo minuto.*

In the year 1305, the Capitano del Popolo of Perugia was Ridolfo Varrani, who at the same time was seigneur of Camerino, his birthplace. In the public records of the Town *Diversorum Annorun* in the few councils that took place, the Priori were already appointed and ten in number, two from each gateway to the city, in substitution of the Consuls of the Guilds. But the year in which they were appointed is not mentioned and the way in which they were chosen also lacks, as does the moment when the Consulate was cancelled, and the way in which the Priori came to power. We can neither explain it nor explain its reasons...And it was established that these ten Priori must live during their office (two months) in the Palazzo which was built for them, and they lived using the public finances and not at their homes as the Consuls had done.

With these same words, Pompeo Pellini, historian and chancellor of the Commune of Perugia in the second half of the 1500s, narrated the creation of the magistracy of the Priori and the institutional revolution that occurred in Perugia at the beginning of the 1300s. The title of Priore, retraceable to other communes such as Florence, was not completely new for Perugia because in the years 1257-1259 a Priore and a College of the Elders collaborated with the Podestà and the Capitano del Popolo in the city government.

But this Priory, established in 1303, appeared and acted as a pivot to a totally new system, originating from a mini 'revolution' inside the government of the people. The figure of the Priori remained, apart from the years 1540-1552, up until 1816, showing clear evidence of the validity and adaptability of this magistracy. The statute in early Italian language of 1342 laid down the election criteria and the duties of the Priori. From this we learn that the office of the Priori lasts for two months (later three months), they were in number of ten, two from each part of the city (two from the merchant guilds and the representatives of the remainder rotated). The Priori had to be at least twenty-five years old, must come from Perugia or its *contado*. They must own a house of a value of at least two hundred liras and a cadastral patrimony of at least one hundred liras and, last but not least, they must have been members of a guild for a minimum of five years. Their duty, as we can read in the statutes, is that of being responsible for 'the right, peaceful and quiet state of the commune, the populace of Perugia and of its *contado*'. This signifies favouring peace in the city and the collaboration between the various officials of the Commune, especially the Podestà and Capitano del Popolo, superintending the good administration of finance and of the communal goods, authorizing the expenses or outgoings of the Commune, and administering directly some of the expense items (processions, guards, messengers and spies, and ambassadors). Amongst their responsibility was that of convening the various councils deciding the matters for the agenda and that of implementing, together with the Podestà and Capitano, the rulings of the councils. But from the statutes we can infer the strong political stance of the magistracy of the Priori which 'guaranteed consensus between the Guilds, protecting them from the aristocracy and acting as an intermediary to the judicial authorities.'

The Council of the Priori had the collaboration of the Council of the Chamberlains of the Guilds, made up of one member from each guild plus four from the merchant guilds and two from the money lenders. Several communal offices of a certain importance depended directly from these two councils, the financial office administered by the Massari to which in the middle of the 1300s the Conservatori della Moneta was added. The statute of 1342 laid down that the Priori 'and their notary had to use the Palazzo del Popolo as their residence both night and day, they had to live in it and never leave it, if not for an evident or necessary reason'.

Many Noblemen, but no Overall Lord...

The 1300s is for Perugia a century of great change, innovation, and progress from many points of view, but it is also the century in which the city became the setting for fierce internal conflicts between two factions, the Raspanti and the Beccherini, who fought a bitter power struggle. The Raspanti faction, made up almost entirely of families from the *popolo grasso,* who were in power, defended their position looking after their own interests. In the other camp was the faction of the Beccherini, the noblemen, who were tenaciously attached to the privileges that their social class guaranteed them, but at the same time they were eager to recapture the hegemonic role held before the advent of the government of the Priori. In order to take power all was permitted, from promoting turmoil to the murder of members of the rival faction, from exile to seizing their property.

Several leading figures took advantage of this situation of continuous conflict, to achieve a leading role: Biordo Michelotti, commander of a group of mercenaries and member of an aristocratic family of Perugia which sided with the popular faction; Braccio Fortebracci a very competent nobleman and seigneur from 1416 to 1424; further – although of a different standing – Giangaleazzo Visconti (1400-1402) and Ladislao di Durazzo, King of Naples (1408-1414). According to Maire Viguer, in all cases they were all regimes of seigniories, while Mineo used for Biordo and Braccio the definition of 'limited seigniory systems' , especially if compared to the custom in the Po Valley and owing to the fact that they commenced in a period of strong political conflict, so as to appear as 'temporary and traumatic regimes generated from the political conflict'. The same could be said for the crypto-seigniory of the Baglioni family clan. It is important to underline that the abovementioned characters, who will be mentioned often in the following pages, had to take into account the fact that Perugia was a Papal dominion, although in this period the capital of the Papal State had been moved to Avignon (1309-1378) and this distance increased the importance of the city in the Duchy, and the government of the Priori had continued the policy of enlargement of the *contado* begun in the 1200s. During the period that the Papal seat was in Avignon, an important event came about for Perugia and the Papal lands: the mission in Italy of the Papal legate, Egidio Albornoz, an important political and military figure, entrusted by Pope Innocent VI to recover the cities 'in flight' from the control of the Church. From 1353 to 1367, he continued in his intent, by diplomatic or military means according to the circumstances. He had most difficulty with Perugia, due to the fact that the city, despite the presence of the legate, continued its expansionism halted though in 1367 by fighting. Albornoz's death came some months later, and prevented the Church from reaping the benefit of the victory. Heedless of the fact that the city was besieged by the Church's allies (*fideles*), and of the fact that the city was economically impoverished and militarily humiliated, the Priori did not intend to surrender, on the contrary they came to an agreement with Bernabò Visconti who at that time was an enemy of the Papal State but at the same time a troublesome ally. The aristocratic faction, kept outside the government of the Priori, took advantage of this difficult situation to try to regain power with the help of the Pope, to whom the city was promised after an agreement or better a conspiracy that was though discovered in the nick of time, and the noblemen involved were executed or exiled. This provoked the immediate reaction of Pope Urban V who took revenge with an interdiction on the city. Perugia was hastily abandoned by Visconti who feared a chain reaction, and thus the city government was forced to sign a peace treaty with the Pope, signed in Bologna in 1370. This brought to a close a period of evident independence and was the beginning of a new period of subjection, contested, difficult and all told without continuity. While ordering the return of the exiled noblemen, Pope Gregory XI elected as Vicar the Cardinal of Bourges, who was 'an Albornoz in miniature as far as intelligence was concerned, but for tyranny and treachery he was five times the latter'. This election provoked a strong opposition from the popular government, which was not that united, because the *popolo minuto* and the rest of the lower classes, who had suffered from the war and from the consequent famine and who were instigated by the aristocracy, urged the Council to permit the Cardinal to enter the city, because he had promised food and cereals. The turmoil that followed opened the gates of Perugia to the first ecclesiastical dictatorship and allowed the return of the aristocracy to power. Thus the popular government was overcame by the joint action of the Papal States, noblemen and *popolo minuto*, and recovered its power only as a reaction to the tyrannical dictatorship of the Papal Vicar, Gerardo du Puy, abbot of Monmaggiore, whose administration can be summarized by a series of drastic and unpopular measures such as the construction of the Cittadella di Porta Sole, a true fortress symbol of the papal rule over the city. The unavoidable and consequent rebellion of the city forced the Abbot's flight at the end of 1375. This turmoil was part of a wider movement of popular rebellion against the Papal representatives, known as the War of the 'Otto Santi' (Eight Saints). Immediately after the abbot's flight the hated symbol of the papal power was dismantled, the fortress, and also the alliance between aristocracy and commoners made during the fight against the Vicar came to an end. In 1377 the noblemen hatched a plot that, once discovered, drove into exile most of them and gave new vigour to the popular government which in any case was destined to profound internal tension when the Michelotti, an important family in Perugia sided with the commoners, attempted to make an agreement with the Anjou in order to return Perugia to the Pope. Their expulsion weakened the popular government and allowed the noblemen to achieve once again a position of strength taking over the control of the main city offices and in fact exercising power. The final exclusion of the populace occurred only in 1389 following a violent turmoil headed by a member of the Baglioni family. Killed or exiled the Raspanti, the noblemen created the Magistracy of 'Cinque dell'Arbitrio' which for a certain period collaborated with the Priori in the city government.

But the aristocratic regime did not have an easy life, besieged from outside by the exiled and inside by the difficult economic situation – they had depleted the public funds –

and by the discontent of the city populace due to the continual suffering from famine and epidemics. They tried to make a treaty, and because of this in 1392 Pope Boniface IX was invited to visit the city in the capacity of an authoritative peacemaker, on which the Pope took the power in his hands and those of his delegates, after which he obtained the consent of the noblemen and the commoners for the return of those exiled. This agreement did not last for long, one month later a violent turmoil provoked a new expulsion of the noblemen and a headlong flight of the Pope. The reborn popular government immediately took over all institutional power, this time under the protection of Biordo Michelotti, the captain of an army of mercenaries who thanks to his fame as captain and to the popular tradition of his family, exercised for a short period a 'coverted' seigniory on the city, without damaging in any way the framework of the government. Shortly afterwards, a plot hatched by his brother in law, the abbot of San Pietro, Francesco Guidalotti, brought his power to an end and he was assassinated. This was the right moment for the noblemen to return to the city, this they did shortly afterwards.

But Perugia was entering, against its will, into a wider political ball game with reduced freedom of manoeuvre. The protagonists of this game were, in this period, on the one side the Papal Seat – although troubled by the Great Scism did not renounce to the control over the city, on the other side was Giangaleazzo Visconti, Duke of Milan, who after having subdued by political means, financial means or by arms most of Northern Italy, turned his attention to central Italy and found in Perugia a possible strong base from where to begin his plan to unify central and northern Italy. Tenacious opposition was made by Florence, being itself in a period of expansion, and fearful of losing its supremacy in central Italy, but above all it was careful not to be encircled by Visconti. Thus the control of Perugia was of vital importance also for the Florentine Republic, but the Milanese diplomacy and the promise of substantial financial help brought the Commune of Perugia into Visconti's arms. On January 19th 1400, the Priori deliberated the subjection of the city to the Duke of Milan who put all the local administration under the control of his officials. But they accepted the demands of the Priori to maintain their residence in the Palazzo 'as was custom at the time', and to maintain untouched statutes, laws and regulations of the Commune, and in conclusion to retain the Studio, which was on the contrary reinforced by the Duke thanks to an extraordinary donation of two thousand florins. At the same time Visconti painted his coat of arms, displaying a snake, in several copies and in several locations on the Palazzo dei Priori.

The unexpected death of Giangaleazzo Visconti, after only two years of his rule, brought back Perugia under the control of the Church, but in June 1408 a new seignior installed himself in the city, Ladislas the Magnanimous, King of Naples. The reason for this was that Braccio Fortebracci da Montone was in the King's pay; he was a captain of a troop of mercenaries well-known in the Italian panorama, who since that April had been in Umbria putting to rout the troops of the weak government of the Raspanti. Fear of falling into the captain's arms, led the popular government to make a secret treaty with Ladislas, on the condition that he kept outside the city the exiled aristocracy. The King accepted and became seignior of the city, forbidding the return of the exiled.

The experience with Giangaleazzo and Ladislas was the exact opposite to that with Biordo and Braccio, these latter deeply rooted in the local history, politically involved in it even though with different alliances, but soldiers capable of creating wide alliances and coalitions. In fact Braccio, despite the subjection of Perugia under Ladislas, did not abandon Umbria, for revenge against what he considered treason by the King of Naples but also because meanwhile he had entered in the service of the Church. He went throughout the *contado* plundering and attempting in all ways to weaken Perugia's defensive system, this became the major objective of his military activity. In 1414, the unexpected death of Ladislas relit the hopes of the noblemen whose dream came true in July 1416, when Braccio, after having defeated the popular army in a very violent and bloody battle in Sant'Egidio, entered Perugia triumphantly, contributed firstly to the return of the exiled noblemen and thus provoked a transition in the administration of power, even though the political administrative structures of the Commune did not change and the Priori continued to hold the same positions. With a public ban, Braccio guaranteed the inhabitants of Perugia that he would maintain both the ordinary magistracies, including Priorato and Camerariato, and the statutes, excluding important cases of public order. A clever move that had the intention of presenting his 'reign' as the natural prosecution of the Republican and Communal government. But the real facts were different, because Braccio gathered all the power in his hands or, during his absence, in those of his lieutenant. Besides this, and in order to weaken the popular party, he laid down that any inhabitant of Perugia of whatsoever social class and condition must be admitted into the Colleges of the Guilds, without paying taxes. He wanted to favour both the aristocracy who were not involved in business and thus they were excluded, and the *popolo minuto* who had not enough money to pay the admission tax. Finally, Braccio, via his supporters, guaranteed a continuous control on the Communal life. From this base, he intended to rule over Perugia and give it that peace and quiet that all the populace expected, being tired of the continuous internal conflicts. And in fact, under Braccio's rule the turmoil came to an end. The last foolish ambitions of the Raspanti were swept away around about the year 1416, when a rebellion headed by the Michellotti family clan was put down and, taking advantage from this incident, Braccio exiled the hostile family. It is also true that the presence of Braccio in Perugia was sporadic, not only because he was unable to settle down to a quiet life, but above all because he tried to conquer areas over which other seigniors ruled. Braccio Fortebracci's life ended under the walls of L'Aquila where he died during a battle in June 1424. Without success his descendants tried to gather his inheritance, and at the same time other soldiers of fortune directed their gaze on Perugia, including for example Niccolò Piccinino and his sons Francesco and Jacopo, but with little or no success.

After the death of Braccio da Montone the city saw an acceleration in the ascent to power of the Baglioni, already well-known on the political scene. But this ascent was constantly monitored, and often halted and sometimes controlled by the rival families inside the city, and by the Pope and his officials outside.

Perugia Part of the Papal States: Papal Rule, Diarchy and the Baglioni Family as a Tertiary Power

In 1417 with the election of Martin V the great schism came to an end. The Pope had in mind a well prepared programme of how to recover 'his State', but he had to be patient and wait until Braccio's death, which came in 1424, a fact that brought Perugia under the rule of the Church once again. In Perugia the end of Braccio's 'seigniory' gave rise to dramatic tension in the Communal Council between the supporters of the Pope, on the one hand, and Braccio's son, Oddo, on the other. In the end, the pro-Pope faction prevailed, backed by the Baglioni family, which played a leading role in the following events in the history of Perugia. On July 18th of that same year an agreement divided into various articles was signed, this was a sort of convention agreed upon between the Pope and the Commune, with which the Pope obtained complete dominion over the city and its territory. The Pope's conditions were not that demanding, but took into account the fact that Perugia was a powerful Commune with deep-rooted traditions of self-government. As mentioned above, Martin V had a large programme going beyond Perugia, a programme which foresaw a restoration of the Papal States first of all, especially of the provinces created by Pope Innocent III and revised by Albornoz. These Provinces, ruled by a Rector assisted by a Parliament, were situated in the centre of Italy stretching from the Adriatic to the Tyrrhenian Sea, and later Albornoz included: the Marca d'Ancona, the Duchy of Spoleto, Romandiola, Campagna and Marittima (to the south of Rome), and the Patrimonio di San Pietro in Tuscia (to the north of Rome going as far as Orvieto). Pope Martin V made some changes to this scheme, establishing a new district for Perugia which included Lake Trasimeno, Fratta (today Umbertide) and Montone to the north, Città della Pieve and the Chiana area to the west, Marsciano to the south, and Gubbio and Gualdo Tadino to the east. As regards government bodies, the Councils of the Priori and the Chamberlains were confirmed, together with the office of the Podestà, who from then on was elected by the Pope, while the office of the Capitano del Popolo disappeared for about thirty years. The statutes and the residence of the Priori in the same Palazzo were also confirmed as they were. The central power ruled over the political sphere with two key officials who were part of the new order: the Legate and the Governor, and in the financial sector with the Apostolic Treasurer, an office that was already existent in the past, but from then on was strengthened. In Perugia, the direct representative of the Pope was the Legate (usually a cardinal, but often substituted by a Vice Legate or the Governor) who lived in the area where the communal palazzi stood, on one side of the square between the Cathedral and the Palazzo dei Priori. This high official dictated the guidelines of the general policy, especially foreign policy, controlled the local magistracies, levied special taxes, enacted edicts and announcements, and listened to the appeals of proceedings.

In the case of Perugia, the overlap between communal bodies and papal officials created a cohabitation rightly defined by the word 'diarchy', a government where the relationships varied according to the power and the unity of the communal powers or the strength of character of the legate. In any case it was a difficult and troublesome cooperation with a third power attempting to impose their personal rule over the city, the Baglioni family. The diarchic system of Perugia had a very critical juncture in the creation of the *borse*. The *borsa* or *sacco* was a list of names of those inhabitants who were entitled to hold public office. It was drawn up every five years by a committee of *insaccolatori*. Names were drawn by lot, or openly, whenever there was a need to allocate a post. The whole electoral system was run by the *borsa*, and it is not surprising that there was a dispute between the Papal States, that wanted the list to be done in Rome and then sent to Perugia, and the Commune that wanted the list to be drawn up in Perugia and only afterwards approved by the Legate, who certainly was more easily influenced because he lived in the city. This balance of power, ever mobile, tipped the scales in favour of the commune's or Pope's wishes, depending on the resistance that Perugian authorities were able to build up. These authorities, for their part, could rely on strong and resolute allies like the Baglioni family. This family was one of the twelve families that represented the ruling aristocracy in the city: the Oddi, Ranieri, Signorelli, Tei, della Corgna, Arcipreti della Penna, Montevibiani, Armanni della Staffa, Montesperelli, Montemelini, Alfani and the aforementioned Baglioni families. Even though there were not many of them, this still could not guarantee agreement between the noble families, especially due to the hegemonic ambitions of the house of Baglioni, which was itself rather divided. This situation caused friction, hatred, turmoil and even bloody feuds which involved the whole city and offered the Popes a reason to intervene, in order to restore peace (the declared aim), and to exert pressure (as happened). This happened, for example, in 1486, when, in order to restore peace in the city, Pope Innocent VIII decided upon a series of constitutional reforms, and together with them the Pope relocated the *borsa* to Rome itself. The Pope's decision found strong opposition only from Guido and Ridolfo Baglioni, the heads of the family clan in that period, because the other leading families sided with the Pope. The turmoil did not end with the

Pope's intervention; on the contrary, it intensified and magnified the well-known malaise in Perugia, ending in the autumn of 1488 in a violent fight between the Baglioni and their main rivals, the Oddi, a fight that soon got out of control, an outright war waged by both parties with fierce energy. They fought inside and outside the walls, up until the complete defeat of the Oddi family and their allies, killing or exiling the male members of these families. Then an emergency magistracy was created, called the 'Dieci dell'Arbitrio' (controlled by the Baglioni), an extraordinary magistracy but not entirely new, because it had already been convened in the past during short crisis periods. This magistracy had authority for defence, the recruitment of soldiers, the maintenance of law and order, defence of the city from the exiles, and day to day city administration.

Without any doubt, the Baglioni were the most important family in Perugia and modelled the political characteristics of the second half of the 15th century and after. They owned vast tracts of land and castles received as feuds from the popes as a compensation for their military services. They also were in good relations with the Medici family, esteemed mercenaries by the Italian powers, and skilled in creating alliances and relationships through an acute policy of marriages, that said they were rightly the third force between the communal government and the papal representatives. The high offices held in the city (members of the 'Consiglio dei Priori', of the 'Dieci Savi dello Studio', ambassadors and intermediaries) together with the prestige built up outside the city allowed them to crown themselves as city paladins, and to negotiate with the Pope's representatives almost as equals. Beside this, they also carried out a family strategy aimed at a personal rule over the city, a power that some historians have interpreted as a 'covert seigniory', and others as a 'leading role' inside a small aristocratic oligarchy of the city.

Between 1488 and 1500, the Baglioni family increased their power. The older brothers Guido and Rodolfo, Malatesta's sons, controlled together the political life, while their sons (Astorre, Gismondo, Giampaolo, Adriano, Marcantonio, Simonetto and Ottaviano) were mercenary captains for several states of the peninsula, and were in Perugia only occasionally. The exiled members of the Oddi family made numerous attempts to return inside the walls, but the Baglioni family were never caught unawares, thanks to the fact that they could rely on 2,500 soldiers. But the dynasty had an intrinsic vulnerability that came from the unflinching controversy between the principal branch of Malatesta's sons and the secondary branches. From this point of view the year 1500 proved to be decisive. A plot, supported by the Duke of Camerino, was organized by Filippo di Braccio, Carlo, known as Barciglia from a secondary branch of the Baglioni family, Grifonetto of Braccio's family line, and by Girolamo degli Arcipreti. The opportunity came with the marriage between Astorre di Guido Baglioni and Lavinia Colonna, when all the members of the main branch of the family were gathered together. During the night between July 14th and 15th, while Astorre was still guest of Grifonetto, the slaughter took place, in which Astorre, Simonetto, Gismondo and Guido were killed, while Rodolfo and Giampaolo survived. Giampaolo, escaped to Deruta. He immediately organized an insurrection, then assaulted the city and won over the conspirators. During the fight Grifonetto perished, and his mother Atalanta commissioned Raphael the painful *Deposition from the Cross* that, after being the altar piece in the family chapel in San Francesco al Prato, today is at the Galleria Borghese in Rome.

The years 1501-1503 marked the supremacy of Giampaolo who had connections with Cesare Borgia, but escaped from his mortal embrace. He created a sort of triumvirate, called Defenders of the Papal State of Perugia, with his father and his cousin, Adriano, but the most serious risk came from his same family due to the rivalry with the other members of the family, especially with his cousin Gentile, bishop of Orvieto, who obtained the dispensation to return to the lay state, and was very ambitious. The accession to the papal throne of Julius II and his policy detrimental to the seigniories of the Papal States created serious problems for Giampaolo and induced him to make a formal act of submission in order to maintain his standing. Thus, when in 1506 the Pope entered the city, he was deferentially welcomed by Giampaolo Baglioni, a fact that was strongly criticized by Niccolò Machiavelli. The Pope first of all dissolved the magistracy of the 'Dieci dell'Arbitrio' – re-established in 1503 by Giampaolo – gave his Legate the control of finance, definitively passed to higher authorities in Rome in 1512, and limited the supremacy of the Baglioni family by permitting their rivals to return to the city and re-creating that equilibrium inside the oligarchy which was traumatically broken by the expulsion of the Oddi in 1488. The successor of Pope Julius II, Leo X Medici, was not satisfied by that renewed and instable equilibrium, but expected Giampaolo to adhered to the interests of the Pope and the Medici family. Thus, when he came to suspect the existence of an agreement between Giampaolo Baglioni and the Duke of Urbino, he did not hesitate to assassinate the former and to re-affirm decidedly the control of the Church over Perugia. Giampaolo's death gave rise to a bloody feud inside his family, with fierce personal revenge coming to the fore. In this period, one of Giampaolo's sons, Malatesta, came into the limelight, and in 1529 accepted the office of General Governor of the Florentine troops. His election increased the already existing friction between Perugia and Pope Clement VII, member of the Medici family exiled from the Florentine Republic, towards whom and during the first year of war Malatesta was loyal, carrying out audacious and timely military action. But later, his playing for time and, above all, his agreement with the Prince of Orange, commander in chief of the Imperial forces allied with the Pope, made to save the city of Florence from plunder, cast a shadow over his loyalty, so much so that as reward the Pope gave him a pardon together with new properties and privileges. On September 11th 1530, Malatesta entered Perugia, nevertheless triumphantly, and then he retired to his estate in Bettona where he died in 1531.

His death led to a further change of mind of the Pope who, soon afterwards, banished his son Rodolfo II and nephew Giampaolo II (Orazio's son), on the contrary he allowed entrance into the city again to Braccio, who was the head of the rival faction. This situation lasted up until Pope Clement VII's death (1534). The new Pope, Paul III Farnese, attempted to broker a settlement between the rival factions, but unsuccessfully. Rodolfo II took advantage of this situation to enter again the city at that moment without defence, sack-ing it and killing the Vice-Legate together with one of the Priori and the Chancellor. During the night the Palazzo del Legato (ex Communal Palazzo) was set on fire, and burnt to the ground together with the adjoining Palazzo del Vescovado. Paul III, faced with these serious incidents, banished the Baglioni family from the city and from their properties, and ordered them to disband their army. They abided by the order: Rodolfo left Perugia and put himself at the service of Alessandro de' Medici. But the long-lasting disorders continued, and the appointment of a commissary became necessary. In September, a personal visit by the Pope became advisable, and during the stay of the Pope some magistracies were reformed and garrisons were established for the city defence. The situation deteriorated due to the continual financial difficulties of the Papal States, determined by the ever increasing needs of a State with modest finances in comparison to its vast foreign policy commitments, such as the wars against Spain, the Turks and the Protestants which increased heavily the military expenses. That all led as a consequence to the renewed imposition of several extraordinary taxes as, for example, the chimney tax, and the increase of others like the salt tax, which the Apostolic Chamber controlled. In 1537, Perugia refused to pay the tribute on the family units, and asked for a reduction in the salt tax, but without success. The fact that the Pope refused to come to terms led to a decisive reaction by the inhabitants of Perugia. They placed a crucifix above the door of the cathedral, in front of which the Chancellor of the Commune, Mario Podiani, delivered a seditious speech to his fellow inhabitants. On March 17th 1540, Pope Paul III declared the city insurgent, interdicted it and excommunicated its inhabitants, after which he prepared to send military forces there. The inhabitants of Perugia made a last attempt, they called back Rodolfo Baglioni, who – to tell the truth – hesitated considering the battle lop-sided, but in the end he accepted to return to the city, also due to the pressures from Cosimo I who threatened the expansionist strategy of Paul III in central Italy. On May 16th Baglioni engaged the Pope's soldiers in several skirmishes but, due to a meagre food supply and finances, he decided to make a treaty with Pierluigi Farnese, Duke of Castro and commander in chief of the papal army, for the surrender of the city, safeguarding the lives and the goods of the local inhabitants. On June 13th Rodolfo Baglioni left Perugia and two days later Pierluigi Farnese, the Pope's nephew, entered the city together with his troops. On July 25th the ambassadors of Perugia went to the Pope to ask for his pardon, that was given *ab omnibus penis spiritualibus*, but a new destiny was already waiting: Pierluigi settled in the city, and immediately began planning the construction of a Rocca, or rather the building of a fortress to be commissioned from 'Messer Antonio da San Gallo'. This was to be built in that same area that in the past had been the site of the Baglioni properties. In this way, a new building completely re-designed the heart of the old town centre inserting in the medieval urban plan an alien structure, that of the Farnesi. This fortress was adorned with symbolic images of the power and oppression of the papal government, and determined its singular history, which ended with its almost total demolition in the 1800s. New officers were appointed with the building of the Fortress (Captain, Governor and Keeper) and the Priori disappeared from 1540 to 1552, being replaced by a new puppet magistracy in 1542- the 'Conservatori dell'Ecclesiastica Obbedienza' (with black garments instead of purple) – while the Legate maintained its power. Nevertheless this represented the first symptom of a recovery in the relations between Perugia and Rome. The main task of the Conservatori was that of maintaining public order in the city, while the territory as a whole was transferred to the direct financial administration of the Apostolic Chamber. At the same time they started to recall the exiled. The re-organization of the local administration achieved an important target, the re-establishment of the Priori, during the papacy of Julius II, who was related to the local aristocracy through his sister Giacoma who married a member of the della Corgna family. But the return of the diarchy prior to 1540 was only apparent, because the central government intervened decisively on the social and political issues, favouring the rise of wealthy families up until then with less politically influence, and dispersing to distant estates those families who up until then had most political influence, such as the Baglioni. At the same time the expansion of the working middle class was discouraged, a fact that later was to have serious consequences, making the Papal States a backward region when compared to other states.

A number of Popes from Paul IV (1555-1559) to Clement VIII (1592-1605) developed the administrative system, amongst whom Sixtus V (1586-1590) who left his mark and made in many ways a definitive re-organization of the State and of his papacy. He played the role of a king who continued the policies of his predecessors and took them to the extreme, adopting a personal style of government (the Pope reigned aided only by those loyal to him, cardinal or lay). He already had an important mechanism of control over the territory, the Consulta, which administered that pertaining to food supply, taxes, criminal justice, and even up to the establishment of several magistracies, and which papal officials, such as the governors of the cities and the Legates of the provinces, were dependent on. Furthermore, Sixtus V used to the full the Congregations, permanent offices which had the responsibility for the spiritual and lay governmental affairs of the Church, a responsibility that increased after the Council of Trent. Amongst the Sacred Congregations of the Sistine, several had the responsibility for the spiritual administration of the Church, like the Holy Office and the Sacred Congregations of the Council of Trent and of the Rites, and others were accountable for the lay administration of the State, such as the food board, road construction and maintenance and tax relief. This latter, together with the Consulta, were specifically responsible for defending the various communities of the State from abuses and bad government especially in the fiscal sector.

Pope Clement VIII Aldobrandini continued the tendency of strengthening the central power structure of the state at the expense of the peripheral administrations, surpassing his predecessors and expanding the administration of the Provinces by the creation of a new Congregation, called of the Good Government, which re-organised the communes and regulated their relationship with the central bodies of the State. The jurisdiction of the Good Government expanded to cover all of the communities of the State, including Perugia, excepting Rome, the legations of Bologna, Ferrara, Ravenna, and Forlì.

Their duties required tact, they had to arbitrate on the financial regulations of the Communes and, besides this, undertake the functions of supreme court of first instance and last resort for resolving all the controversies between the Communes and the population on taxes, civic customs and similar. Pope Clement VIII behaved like a monarch who would not tolerate limitation to his authority, enlarging everywhere possible the control of the State. Cities like Perugia, which insisted with its claim to an anachronistic self-government, were the 'most relevant obstacle in the construction of a State'. For this reason, popes like Sixtus V and Clement VIII devoted themselves to reorganising those features within a plan to centralize that included both finance and administration. The results were not that evident, so that the Papal States could not be considered 'a State in the modern sense', instead 'up until its end it was made up of states' over which the pope reigned 'as a prince amongst the other Italian princes'.

An Enduring Sleep and the Signs of a Fragile Re-Awakening

The 1600s and the 1700s were centuries of administrative stabilization for the Papal States. Especially in the 1600s, Umbria appeared as a multifaceted area and, partly, an expedient, but certainly more clear cut and established than in the past. Several important feudal jurisdictions disappeared, like the 'State of the Baglioni' in the vicinity of Bettona, while the vicissitudes of the Guerra di Castro overwhelmed the Duchy of

Castiglione del Lago and Chiugi founded by Pope Julius II for his della Corgna nephews. In the Umbrian Legation, the authority of the Provincial Governor of Perugia was finally consolidated. The Governor was assigned a broad responsibility, in the judicial system, he had the same position as that of the Podestà in the communal period but with increased right of appeal, and as to authority that of the Priori of the Arts before 1540, including the right to convene and dissolve the city councils, and the right to participate at the meetings ratifying the resolutions. The Governor received directives from Rome and, if necessary he had to transmit them to the Priori. Further, this high official also was the executor of the privileges granted by the pope to the city. Several Governors, even though elected for a short period of time, participated in the cultural life of the city (in the Academies) or in the religious one (in the Confraternities), and the city granted citizenship to several Governors, which was a sort of 'pledge', an understanding that these illustrious characters, once returned to the Curia, would continue to defend the local interests as 'patrons'.

The final inclusion of Perugia and its territory in the Papal States led to an inevitable withdrawal into the city with a consequent exit from the Italian and international trade network. The local upper classes, who were identified with the aristocracy, always focused their interests on landed property, which was considered a source of income as well as an investment. Three different categories characterized the aristocracy in Perugia: 'absentee' administrators of their properties, legal profession, and an evident aristocratic lifestyle. From this point of view, the aristocracy focused its attention on the 'Palazzo' as a perfect city residence, so that between the inclusion of Perugia in the Papal States and the Unification of Italy, the urban plan notably changed due to the construction of many noble palazzi, which were situated in the most prestigious areas of the city. The palazzi were a tangible sign of the social and economic reputation of the family as a whole, and were lived in by their servants. Here, they collected paintings and different artistic objects. Here they lived, and intertwined relationships with inhabitants of the same social class. Here, they organized a grandiose and exclusive social life, with banquets, parties, concerts and theatrical performances. For these latter, special structures were constructed and served also as meeting places for wealthy people. There were two public theatres constructed in the 1700s inside the city: the theatre of the Pavone which was patronized by the aristocracy, and the Theatre of the Verzaro patronized by the rising bourgeoisie, later dedicated to the local composer Francesco Morlacchi, well-known also as the director of the Italian Opera in Dresden.

Often the palazzi were built from scratch, but more often they were the result of unification, demolition, enlargement and embellishment of medieval buildings that had belonged to merchants and artisans, originally high and narrow. These buildings after the necessary building works were turned into palazzi with more than one floor, and ennobled with decorations, main doors and other elements that gave them the appearance of a unique building, such as Palazzo Baldeschi (Piazza della Repubblica), and Palazzo Friggeri (Piazza IV Novembre). On the other hand, there also were palazzi built completely from scratch, such as Palazzo Bourbon di Sorbello in Piazza Piccinino, Palazzo Connestabile della Staffa at Porta Sole (today seat of the Augusta Town Library), Palazzo Antinori later Gallenga Stuart (today seat of the University for Foreigners), the Palazzi Della Penna (exhibition area and seat of the Committee for Umbrian Local History), Aureli Manzoni in Piazza Morlacchi (Faculty of Humanities and Philosophy), and Palazzo Donini (seat of the Regional Council). In contrast to the ascendancy of the aristocracy, there was a progressive impoverishment of those inhabitants who were no longer engaged in business activities, together with their exclusion from the central areas of the town and their consequent transfer to the nearby *borghi* –

especially next to Porta San'Angelo and Sant'Antonio – and to the rural environs. At that time there was also the necessity to care for the poor and infirm, and to this end local buildings were used, like the hospice next to the church of San'Egidio del Nobile Collegio della Mercanzia restored in the 16th century (Corso Garibaldi), together with the large city hospice of Santa Maria della Misericordia which for more than three centuries had occupied a vast area with its factories, going from Via della Peschiera (now Oberdan) to Piazza del Sopramuro. Only in 1921, was it transferred to the area occupied by the Convent of Santa Maria di Monteluce, a concession made by the Commune in 1910.

As regards religious architecture, a church in particular stood out, the church and monastery of San Filippo Neri (better known as *Chiesa Nuova*) whose construction began in 1627 on a design by the Roman architect Paolo Maruscelli, while, in 1740, the Olivetans moved into the new large monastery of Monte Norcino Nuovo designed by Carlo Murena with the beautiful church designed by Luigi Vanvitelli. On the wish of the French Government the university was transferred to this building.

The Jacobean and Napoleonic adventures were particularly significant for Perugia, because the city was encouraged to leave behind the dreariness of the papal government, into which later on it fell once again.

In February 1798, during the march to Rome to establish there a Republic, General Berthier reached Perugia where he found the local Jacobeans ready to welcome the French troops, occupy the Fortress abandoned after the flight of the papal troops and ready to proclaim a Republic. The French created a centralized Municipality, in which the nobleman Fabio Danzetta and the well-known doctor and intellectual Annibale Mariotti participated, they were two of the members of a group including exponents of the progressive bourgeoisie and the aristocracy, artisans and commoners, together with numerous representatives from the church. Important economic measures were immediately adopted, such as the abolition of the tax on flour, the reduction of the prices of salt and bread, and the free circulation of goods and wheat. But this was not enough to pacify the discontent spreading amongst the farmers, who felt threatened by the French occupation and by the expectation of famine and hunger. They were also embittered by the age old hate for the city that was combined with the recent hate towards the Jacobeans (almost all landowners and large tenant farmers), and last but not least they were also worried about the attack against the religious orthodoxy. This situation came to a head with the rebellion known as the 'Disorders of Trasimeno' (1798) which was firstly underestimated and later ruthlessly suppressed. About one year later, between June and July 1799, a violent attack on the city was launched by the Austro-Russian army, which had already defeated the French in northern Italy. Once barricaded in the fortress, the civil and military authorities prepared themselves to resist to the end but, due to a rebellion organized by the supporters of the Papal States, the situation precipitated. The Fortress, last garrison of resistance, surrendered on August 31st. Shortly afterwards, Cardinal Agostino Rivarola arrived from Rome. He was entrusted by the Pope to purge the opposition, the first victim was Mariotti himself, who died in 1801 during his imprisonment. A period of difficult normalisation was soon interrupted from 1805 by a further Napoleonic occupation, and we can say that Perugia lived the various phases of occupation and dissolution of the Papal States in a climate of complete turmoil, up until 1808 when a French military garrison occupied again the Fortress. After which a stable government was established in Perugia, composed of the Jacobeans 'from the beginning', who in the name of the Napoleonic policy of integration became the 'intermediary between the new authority and the ancient aristocracy in Perugia, for whom they endeavoured to maintain a role in the city life, and also in the local administration'. And even though in the new administrative system Perugia played second fiddle to Spoleto in the Trasimeno District, it nevertheless stimulated the leading classes of the city which not only aimed at taking advantage of the situation, but also encouraged a new development of the city, so that the local economy, based almost exclusively on agriculture, was redeveloped thanks to that same influential group of the city, made up of landlords and bourgeoisie engaged, unusually, in commercial and financial activities. Special care was dedicated to the cultivation of grapevines and mulberry-trees, hemp and flax, and to the development of the live stock sector. These were all recommended by the French occupiers and met with the enthusiasm of the leading classes of Perugia. Particular effort was put into the maintenance and the development of roads, mainly 'in order to breach the traditional isolation of the city and renew communications with the countryside'. From the social point of view, the Napoleonic policy of integrating the old and new social classes proved successful. In this period a 'sort of emerging class' ranging from the local notables to the middle class, who all were employed by the State in the public administration and in the army, came into existence and was to be the main protagonist of the future political struggle of the Risorgimento. After the abdication of Napoleon, the papal arms returned in place and the church bells rang to announce the return of the Pope from exile'. The commissaries arrived from Rome to organize the 'Temporary Papal Administration' and the 'hard work' of the restoration began, starting from the already experienced division of the State into Apostolic Delegations, with the intention of "rationalising the various departments of the administrative institutions, integrating the outskirts with the city centre, reconsidering the departments and districts created by the French, that, from a territorial point of view, could have been integrated". Perugia gave the impression of a city that had returned to its ancient torpor and city life became more peaceful after the exciting period of the French dominion. The nobles returned to their old occupations: their landed properties, theatre and social life, while amongst the bourgeoisie appeared the first signs of restlessness, at the beginning limited to heated debates in the cafes and in the chemists' shops (as in the one of Bernardino Tei). 'In the Perugia of the period of the restored papal regime, old and new powers used their energy to try to resolve the day to day problems concerning the fight against hunger and misery, while the long-term programmes, temporarily put to one side, violently re-exploded in 1831'.

The movement for the Italian Unification arose in 1831, encouraged by Mazzini's ideas and in Perugia supported by a group of patriots who became leading figures of this movement in Umbria: Francesco Guardabassi, Reginaldo Ansidei, Nicola and Pompeo Danzetta, Francesco Donini, Ariodante Fabretti, and Domenico Lupattelli, quoting only the most important. Several of them were members of the Masonry which gave an important contribution to the Risorgimento cause. The revolt of 1831 led to the establishment of a temporary Government in the city, made up of members of the liberal party, and the foundation of a Town Guard headed by Francesco Guardabassi. The uprising was immediately repressed with the consequent persecution of the protagonists of the revolt, first of all Francesco Guardabassi who was imprisoned in Castel Sant'Angelo, and later freed due also to the wave of indignation in the Italian and international press. In 1833 in a newly planned revolt several patriots from Perugia took part, amongst whom the Mazzinian Fabretti stood out. He played an important role in the Italian Unification, also at a national level. The election of Pius IX was enthusiastically welcomed in Perugia, due to his promises to start a process of constitutional reforms, which though were partial in nature and arrived late. However, in 1847, the establishment of a Council of State was considered a positive innovation, also because Luigi Donini of Perugia joined this council with moderate liberal ideas. When in 1848 the First War of Independence started, hundreds of volunteers, headed by Antonio Cesarei, left Perugia and all of them distinguished themselves in the subsequent battles. Two more inhabitants of Perugia (Giovanni Pennacchi and Ariodante Fabretti) joined the Constituent Assembly created the day after the flight of the Pope to Gaeta, a fact that favoured the establishment of the Roman Republic, which was characterized by a short and challenging life, and thwarted by Italian and foreign enemies. Its fall from power was a 'heavy blow for the patriots from Perugia' who had participated in its establishment and fought for it, but it was also a heavy blow for the whole Italian revolutionary movement which was forced to exercise patience for a decade, a difficult period for them. Several inhabitants of Perugia were exiled, amongst whom Fabretti, but many remained in the city, continuing to plot secretly in safe places like the Danzetta and Donini villas. In 1859, the Second War of Independence began, and five hundred volunteers from Perugia participated. The city remained without defence, and thus an easy prey for the papal troops which entered the city in order to repress the riot which had broken out on June 14th, and had led to the creation of a provisional Government. Grievously wrong was the violence that accompanied the military action of the Swiss mercenaries of the Pope. Massacres and plunders caused outrage in Italy and especially abroad, at the same time the heroic resistance of the inhabitants of Perugia was acknowledged. On September 14th 1860, the Piedmontese army entered Perugia and finally freed it. The temporary Government – immediately established by the Piedmontese was entrusted to a special commissary, Gioacchino Napoleone Pepoli – issued a series of decrees to modernise the administrative system and revive business in a short period of time. In November a plebiscite decreed the annexation of the city to the new Kingdom, and inaugurated a new season of relations between the Piedmontese Government and the Province characterized by strong government control and a general trend of centralization of power. In December 1860, General Commissary Pepoli gathered together the Provinces of Perugia, Spoleto, Orvieto and Rieti in a general assembly and declared Perugia the capital city of the Province. The protests against this provision, especially from Spoleto and Rieti ex capital cities themselves (but also by Città di Castello and Orvieto asked for independence) did not alter Pepoli's decision, that appeared to 'mirror the moderate Piedmontese policy which found in centralized administration the solution for the newly born State'.

Perugia had naturally all the benefits of being elected administrative capital, a fact that brought all the prestige and privileges of being the seat of the administrative offices of the Province. The major determinant in the choice was 'the political and economic weight of the new ruling class in the city, made up of those who fought against the papal regime as supporters of moderate political ideals and economic liberalism'. Those were men like Francesco Guardabassi, Nicola Danzetta, Reginaldo Ansidei, Zeffirino Faina, and Evelyn Waddington, who were driven to public protest by the urgent problems left behind by the Papal States, such as the severe economic stagnation and the disturbing inactivity not only from the social and cultural point of view but also from the public services point of view. Consequently the task of the Province, as government body, was focused on particular sectors (the same as those of the moderate government policy), such as education, the protection of the cultural heritage, construction and maintenance of roads and railways, and welfare. But progress was made only in some sectors, such as the protection of the artistic heritage, while from initial and summary statistics of 1862 we learn that results were meagre in the welfare sector, which at the time included three hundred and seventy-nine institutes: hospitals, female orphanages, foundling hospitals, nursery schools, grain banks, state pawnshops, savings bank, endowments for public assistance, endowments for dowries, one mental hospital and one poorhouse. The Province focused its attention on several welfare services and endeavoured to develop them but without particular success and above all not in keeping with the 'old and new community needs'. As regards education, according to the existing sources, there was a lack of official intervention to decisively redevelop this sector, nor effort to rectify the underdeveloped educational system of the papal period, which was based on private schools and/or those run by religious congregations. In Umbria, 83,3% of the population was illiterate at the time, most of all in the countryside, and education was almost exclusively limited to the higher social classes. Perugia was a different case because, on the eve of annexation, it could count several primary schools, a secondary school (*liceo*), the university and the Art Academy. In the decade after the Italian Unification fresh energy was given to the development of primary education, not only for children but also for adults in evening sessions, especially through the training of teachers who up until then were almost inexistent. Thus a slow increase in the level of education (also female) took place in all the Province:

from 8,806 primary school students in 1861 to 29,026 in 1866. But the secondary education continued to be a privilege of the upper classes, even though technical education was encouraged in order to develop the professions. Furthermore, several positive results, achieved though with difficulty, were to be found in public works, such as the demolition of the Rocca Paolina, and the creation of a proper road network, which was a necessity for the economic revival.

In the years following the Italian Unification, Perugia was a city where 'the income from landed properties was concentrated, and where the agricultural surplus gathered from the surrounding countryside, such as from the fertile Tiber valley. At the same time Perugia was the capital of Umbria, a role obstinately claimed to the expense of the other cities of the region'. The local community was characterized on the one hand by the strong presence of a landowning class who were very conservative, and on the other hand by a persistence of common views and opinions in the upper and lower classes, in short a homogeneity that created an urban society and a model that lasted for a long time. This model was backed up by beliefs and interests that were strongly supported by the population, as for example the anti-clericalism and the consequent demolition of the Rocca Paolina, or the foundation of associations for social assistance (such as the

Mutual Aid Society for Artists and Labourers in Perugia, founded in 1861 by local notables). All of these associations were administered by the Masonry which achieved a role of 'Chamber of Political Counterbalance' and at the same time organizational pivot of the society, as regards both the institutional and welfare factors (associations for social assistance, clubs and cultural institutions, and the University).

On July 27th 1893, Ulisse Rocchi, a doctor and owner of the weekly democratic magazine 'La Provincia' was elected (or better re-elected) mayor of the city. Ulisse Rocchi's Town Council has been defined as 'the last sign of life in that programme for social cohesion', that is the last attempt at defining a more modern interclass policy, which could cement the social powers of the city'. Rocchi tried to set in motion a moderate transformation, that was a gradual decrease in the influence of the landed classes and a gradual increase in the merchant classes. In order to do this, he undertook large infrastructure projects, such as city lighting, water and tramways. Inevitably these building works necessitated an increase in taxes that gave rise to discontent and tension. Other problems followed: both the aqueduct and the electrical system needed maintenance and partial reconstruction, and the tram network was overcrowded and inadequate. The most serious damage coming from Rocchi's administration was the collapse in that 'community and social cohesion', that all wanted to maintain, breaking up that mutual solidarity between the different social classes, that had existed up until that moment.

Between 1901 and 1902 a new project matured, a conservative project whose advocate was the new mayor, Luciano Valentini, elected on March 22nd 1903. With Luciano Valentini's administration no more space was left for modernization that which had been an important factor of Rocchi's administration. The mayor's plan was to turn Perugia into the 'capital of agriculture'. Of the same opinion was Romeo Gallenga Stuart (Mary Gallenga Stuart's son), who was the new rising star of the conservative party in Perugia and who later became the deputy and undersecretary for government propaganda abroad and the press). He was successful in imposing a development in the production and trade of agricultural products, but without in any way considering social changes in the countryside.

Here, the fatal incidents of the First World War (1915-1918) led to the creation of committees and initiatives supporting the war event. Especially from 1915 the newspaper 'L'Unione Liberale' (whose main financier was Romeo Gallenga Stuart) sided with the interventionist faction, orienting the public opinion which up until then had been undecided. Shortly afterwards the ruinous consequences of the war became evident both on the battle front and in the city; in Perugia (as in Città di Castello, Marsciano and Magione) there were episodes of intolerance against the austerity regulations, but above all demonstrations against the war took place, whose weight was mainly borne by those women, who were working in the place of the men sent to the front. Especially in the new factories which had been established to meet the needs of the war effort, and which needed a workforce. For example the headquarters of SIAMIC (Aeronautical and Mechanical Company in Central Italy) was in Perugia and its factory in San Feliciano sul Trasimeno, a company that built and repaired seaplanes. Between the end of 1917 and the beginning of 1918, the chain of events followed one after another without a break: the Caporetto retreat on October 24th was followed by the victory on the Piave; the Americans entered the war in 1918, and this led to the belief that the final victory was at hand, this victory came in October in Vittorio Veneto. Also in Perugia, with the news of the victory, great enthusiastic demonstrations took place. On November 4[th,] a procession walked along the city streets, headed by Mayor Valentini.

But the post war period was socially tense and problematical. Perugia at the time was characteristically a small city where the landowners, highly conservative, played a fundamental political role, and held back the process of modernization that was starting in Italy in that period. Besides this, the crisis of the post war period due to inflation, unemployment and the deterioration of the conditions in the countryside gave rise to a series of disorders which had as protagonists the female workforce of the Perugina company, the metallurgic workers, and the sharecroppers. This led to the collapse of the already weak equilibrium, based on paternalism that fed the 'political system founded on the prestige of the upper classes and of the deference of the subordinate classes'. The crisis favoured not only the Socialist Party and the Trade Unions, but also the Catholic movement organized in leagues deeply rooted in the area. The Socialist Town Council headed by Ettore Franceschini presented a programme of important social reforms but of a nature difficult to accomplish, and this led to a severe criticism by the political rivals headed by Alfredo Misuri, an erudite bourgeois who had been elected communal councillor in the anti-Bolshevik faction. Misuri was convinced that there was the need to create 'a political group combining all the democratic workers parties' in opposition to the Socialists, but soon sensed the need of broadening his political struggle by siding with the Fascist Party and its action squads. In 1921, the Fascist Party of Perugia was founded, and was made up of nationalists and ex-servicemen, and was successful in the elections of that same year. Especially Misuri had presented himself as the man 'who would restore public order and the institutions', from then on. But, from its foundation, Fascism in Umbria was characterised by internal conflict: Giuseppe Bastianini opposed Misuri. The former was an ambitious employee of humble origins who sided with Mussolini in order to enter Parliament. The preparations for the March on Rome put in the forefront Perugia, which was chosen as seat of the Quadrumvirate and of the Fascist general staff offices, and was presented as 'the capital of the revolution'. Also here, Bastianini played a fundamental role and the newspaper he founded, 'L'Assalto', became the only newspaper in the region, after the 'Unione Liberale' disappeared. The administrative vote of 1923 led to an overwhelming victory for the Fascist Party, and particularly of Bastianini, with a complete absence of opposition, which had not even been able to take advantage of the discontent of the sharecroppers. But the conflict within the Fascist Party did not lack. In Terni Elia Rossi Passaventi, one of the major exponents of local Fascism, was forced to resign as Podestà, because he did not approve with the agreement between the Town Hall and the Società Terni for the use and administration of the water from the Nera and Velino springs. This agreement had also the approval of Mussolini. Thus the fact that Terni became a Province in 1927 was not only seen as a separation from its dependence on Perugia, but also as a means by which the government could control efficaciously the local political class. To this particular end, in Perugia as elsewhere, the figure of the Podestà was fundamental. The Podestà, chosen by Mussolini, was a local administrator elected without the intervention of the party, but by involving in the political administration of the city the more important and trustworthy exponents of the local ruling class. In Perugia the first elected was Oscar Uccelli, and after him Giovanni Buitoni, the owner of the Perugina company. Particularly this latter had the task of tackling the numerous problems of the city, such as services, public building works and culture. Giovanni Buitoni administered the city as if it was a company. He obtained loans and government grants, carried out important public works such as the aqueduct of the Scirca and the Covered Market, approved a new urban plan, established holiday camps and public assistance units. But his administration was too "free and easy" from the financial point of view and the excessive indebtedness of the Town Hall forced him to resign. After him the Podestà that followed concentrated only on the administrative sector. The anti-Fascist movement had a hard life in Perugia, that appeared as the 'cradle of the Fascist revolution', or even better as 'the capital of the Umbrian rural population'. A city where entrepreneurs and business men, landowners and professionals were linked by a sort of alliance to 'freeze the community in Umbria and in Perugia [...] halt any ideas of modernization [...] and block any change in the sharecropping agreement'. In this situation any opposition to Fascism was easily isolated, up until the 1930s when Aldo Capitini returned to Perugia, an extraordinary non-violent intellectual, philosopher, and educator, who organized a network of young intellectuals who joined the popular anti-Fascists, thanks also to the action of Armando Fedeli, head of the Italian Communist Party, who was more than once forced to flee from the city. But their organization was not immediate and limited, and resistance was meagre, even though the anti-Fascism of the youth was evermore oriented towards Communism. In fact, most of the youth who at the time joined the anti-Fascist movement from 1939 to 1942-1943, and in the 1950s, later became the leading group in the PCI.

In 1943 after the fall of the regime, which gave rise to 'moderate demonstrations of popular enthusiasm', things changed quickly. On September 18th the Comitato dei Dodici was established, the first body that gathered together Communists, Socialists, Catholics and several supporters of Capitini. This was the first example of a unitary political body, but without the characteristics of a true

National Liberation Committee (NLC), which was created shortly afterwards on December 2nd. But the NLC had little relevance in the events that followed, because it was both too recently established and lacking a group of local leading inhabitants, owing to the fact that the whole ruling class of Perugia had joined the Fascist Party. This determined a remarkable fragmentation of the partisan activity that was not even able to coordinate its efforts on the eve of the liberation of Perugia. In fact, unlike what had happened in Terni, the city was freed by the Anglo-American troops which entered the city on June 20th 1944. The same Anglo-American allies searched for the leading local class in order to entrust them the administration of the city, but the problems were numerous and also involved the role of the NLC especially as to the traditional idea of 'continuity' in the history of Perugia, the defence of the social order', and the control of the Communist Party. While the NLC had little success due to its limited backing, the SOC (Social Orientation Centre), founded by Aldo Capitini, from July 1944 played an active role in resolving the contemporary problems (water supply, city lighting, municipal street cleaning and refuse disposal service, street re-construction...) and institutional solutions with the foundation of the League of the Umbrian Communes. In the meantime, Perugia was administered by a heterogeneous Town Hall headed by Mayor Adreani initially, and later by Lupatelli up until April 7th 1946, when the elections gave the city the first elective administration of the post war period. In the referendum of June 2nd, Umbria, with its 71,9% of votes, appeared to be the most Republican region of Italy, after the Trentino and Emilia regions.

Agriculture, Industry and Trade up until the Present Day

The city of Perugia was characterized by the presence of an influential and united class of landowners, who also lived outside the communal borders. 'To the bottom of the Tiber valley in the municipalities of Tifernate and Tuderte, and in the fertile hilly area surrounding Lake Trasimeno, here there were the estates of aristocratic families, bourgeois, and the ecclesiastic and charitable institutions of Perugia'. Furthermore in Umbria, and in the Perugia area, a characteristic of the rural estates was sharecropping, as was customary in the whole of central Italy. In Umbria, the sharecropping system was on the one hand the answer to the need for a food supply for a population increasing in number, and on the other hand a solid base for generating new farmland 'in a region where the soil characteristics and the network of rivers made it very difficult to settle stably'. However, the surplus of production had always been limited, too limited to permit landowners to invest substantially. This all determined a 'defence to the bitter end of the sharecropping system and of the traditional order in the rural world' by the landowners who were also the main political and economic figures in the town. Consequently local sharecroppers distinguished themselves in the national panorama for a 'low profile', as their possibility of choice contractually was next to nothing, and their occupation was compared to that of 'ordinary labourers'. In conclusion, the fact that the landowners used to live in the city rather than on their estates is a significant factor in the relationship between sharecroppers and landowners. In the 1800s and before, these latter carried on a short-sighted policy as to the sharecropping contracts, their sole aim being to defend their property, thus they underestimated the internal tensions and invested in neither new machinery nor workforce. In short, the landed properties in the Perugia area were characterized by absenteeism, inactivity, and little or no innovation. The income coming from the land was totally spent in the city or invested elsewhere, no investment was made in the rural areas and this had serious consequences. Thus on the one hand agricultural output continuously decreased and the farmers were ever poorer, on the other hand the consequent decrease in income gave rise to irritation by the landowners. This stagnant situation gave the sharecropper's families hardly enough to live on and a limited income for the owners. A far-sighted and generalized reorganisation of the property-sharecroppers-land-investment equation lacked. These meagre results led to a further transfer of capital to other business activities also outside the region or the state, and a transfer from the countryside to the city of the farmers, who there hoped to find new job opportunities, even thought the city itself, still blocked in an equilibrium from a bygone age, slowed any attempt of industrialization and remained anchored in a 'progression without development in the countryside'.

The Municipality of Perugia after the Unification of Italy counted on an average population of 50,000 inhabitants, who were increasing in number, slowly but continuously ('tranquil demographic dynamics'). The city was the 'point of reference for the agricultural and commercial activities of this area, almost entirely rural', agricultural trading was done twice weekly at the fairly important markets, and industrial enterprise had a diffident dawn, though always linked to agriculture. The industrial activity began later than in the rest of Italy and also later than in Terni, and was very limited for all of the 1900s. Worthy of mention are the Bonucci Wool Mill founded in 1862 in Ponte Felcino next to the Tiber river, and the silkworm plant founded in 1873 and used for the production of silk, whose headquarters were in Corso Garibaldi in Perugia. At the beginning of the 1900s, the Acropolis of Perugia was the location for several business enterprises like Perugina, but shortly afterwards that urban area was considered no longer suitable for any business activity, and a new area was found in Fontivegge next to the station, that was to become the new industrial area. Perugina was transferred to this area, as was the Tobacco Factory and Colussi (which later was transferred to Assisi in order to take advantage of the fiscal benefits given by the Municipality). Not that far from Fontivegge, in the Santa Lucia area, at the end of the 1920s Luisa Spagnoli began a new enterprise in her industrial warehouses. Here angora rabbits were reared. Special production processes turned their coats into the valuable 'Luisa Spagnoli's Angora', also well-known as "Italian Angora". In the economic self-sufficiency regime of the fascist period, this raw material was much appreciated and used for making clothes named after their creator. The quality of the end product guaranteed the firm a rapid development, thanks also to the entrepreneurial skills of one of Luisa's sons, Mario, also the director of Perugina, who between 1942 and 1943 initiated the construction of a modern Spagnoli plant with advanced characteristics. A new small self-sufficient village that was both a factory and a community, a new industrial model in which cohabited production and recreation. A remarkable input to the firm was given by Lino, Mario's son, who began collaborating with the firm in the 1950s and whose aim was to create a larger variety of products, that beginning with his management were distributed with the "Luisa Spagnoli" brand in shops all over Italy.

The 1900s are also the century in which, in the Acropolis, many public and private companies in the service sector began to establish themselves, such as hotels (Hotel Brufani) and banks. In 1911, the Palazzo delle Poste in Piazza Matteotti was built, and Via Fani was enlarged; in 1932 coming from the proposal of Podestà Giovanni Buitoni, the imposing structure of the Mercato Coperto was built, a brick building on more than one floor, 'externally next to the large vault of the Sopramuro and designed with modern criteria as to hygiene and functionality'. In 1931, the administration announced a national competition to produce a plan for 'urban development'. Alfio Susini in his urban plan tracked the already existent trend of city development to the south, in the direction of the Station, and constructed an orbital road. The city centre, the Acropolis abandoned by business, continued to have all the same well-organized accommodation facilities, even thought not that visible and linked to the Italian University and the University for

Foreigners, this latter was founded in 1921 as the seat for foreign students who were studying the Italian language and culture, and now has also become the seat for degree courses for Italian students. The presence of two universities has been a true resource for Perugia, especially from the 1960s and 1970s when the courses increased in number, and consequently the urban layout of the city changed.

From the end of the Second World War, the rather disorderly proliferation of business activity and of new residential buildings 'began to link together old and new city areas, a fact that the town-planning scheme of 1931 tried to avoid', and imposed on the Commune the creation at the beginning of the 1950s of a General Urban Plan (1956), to which was added a variation in 1962. This urban plan included the protection of the old city centre and the construction of car parks around the same city centre, the increase and development of parks, the construction of residential areas in the city environs, the development on the outskirts of the city centre of the law courts and relative offices and the hospital. This latter in particular has been built recently in the area of San Sisto (the inauguration took place in March 2009) and resulted in the transfer of the Santa Maria della Misericordia Hospital which had been situated in Monteluce, since 1923.

In conclusion, in the Fontivegge area – freed from the Perugina Company from the 1960s (of which only the chimney remains as an example of industrial archaeology) – the offices of the Regione Umbria were transferred together with other administrative offices in the early 1990s. These are gathered together in the 'Broletto', the public administrative building par excellence overlooking a square (named of the 'Bacio') with a fountain, a theatre and residential buildings. The 'Broletto' and the administrative offices continue to be linked to the Acropolis by an escalator passing through the Rocca Paolina and by the Minimetró, an underground characterized by covered and banked tracks linking together the areas of Pian di Massiano and of the stadium to the Acropolis.

SMALL BUT IMPORTANT TOWNS

As in other parts of the region, Assisi is both a city founded by the Umbri and at the same time closely linked to the Etruscans, at least up until the battle of Sentino in 295 BC, the date of the final defeat of the Etruscans by the Romans. As a Roman *municipium* (district), *Asisium* was prosperous, and the temple of Minerva was clear evidence of this, with its fluted columns and Corinthian capitals, overlooking the modern Piazza del Comune. Assisi itself underwent an assault by Totila, King of the Goths, and was plundered by his troops; like Perugia and other cities, it had Byzantine garrisons, and for this very reason was heavily and continuously attacked by the Lombards, who included it within their Duchy of Spoleto. The Commune, established in the 12th century (a first mention of it dates to 1140), was in contact (its independence was recognized in 1160) with, and in conflict (it was besieged) with, Emperor Frederick I who had sent the archbishop of Mainz to Italy in order to halt the self-governing tendency of the Communes, which included Assisi, which underwent a violent occupation in 1174 by Konrad of Urslingen, Duke of Spoleto, who was a key figure in the military and territorial policy over the peninsula by the Swebians, but at the same time a troublesome figure. After his fall, in 1198 Assisi was also included in the area of the Papal States, and came under the protection of Pope Innocent III, in particular. Between the 12th and 13th century, the Commune of Assisi developed its institutions (as in the other communes). This development had its founding point in the pact of 1210 between 'Majors' and 'Minors', at the end of a period of internal and external conflicts with the ruling Perugia (one need only mention the defeat of Assisi's troops, where the future St Francis was also present, in 1209). As regards government bodies, Assisi moved from a Council of Consuls to a Podestà, between 1225 and 1230; around about this same period, the office of Capitano del Popolo was established, and a Palazzo was built in the square specially for this office. The conflict between Frederick II and Pope Gregory IX involved Assisi, which embraced the pro-Guelph faction. The city was besieged by Saracen troops led by Vitale d'Aversa, who were halted by the famous intervention of Santa Chiara, who in that period was in San Damiano. Furthermore, the history of the city was characterized by frequent bellicose relations with Perugia, which tried to include it under its rule, but it was also marked by remarkable internal friction, which can be identified with two families and two political factions: a Ghibelline family, De Nepis, 'from the Upper Town', and a Guelph family, the Fiumi, 'from the Lower Town'. The conflict between these two factions was a very serious problem that influenced the whole history of the city. The in-fighting, and the desire to govern, of both the 'upper' and 'lower' parts of the city gave rise to continuous political instability, and inevitably opened the door to attempts, almost always ruinous and short-lasting, to bring in a seigniory government. In this period, Muzio di Francesco crowned himself paladin, and leader of the exiled Ghibellines, and favoured their return to Assisi by force of arms, and thanks to his merits he was elected seignior, albeit for a short period, which stormily and dramatically ended with his excommunication, and the total interdiction of the city. After this short period as a seigniory, Assisi came back within the orbit of Perugia – never a stable situation, and in fact one that was always full of friction – so much so that when Albornoz arrived in Italy the city took advantage of this situation, but inevitably fell under a different sphere of influence, the sphere of the Papal States and of their representative cardinal, who reconstructed the Rocca previously demolished by Urslingen. However, Perugia did not give in, and, taking advantage of the internal conflicts and the desire to achieve political power, on the part of figures like Guglielmo di Carlo, used this latter personage to force its way to dominance among the rival factions, and 'reconquered' the city. Biordo Michelotti, a member of a Perugia family linked to the 'people's' faction, also took advantage of this conflict between rival factions, and after his death his son Ceccolino, along with Giangaleazzo Visconti, as seignior of Perugia, Guidantonio da Montefeltro and Braccio da Montone followed suit. The list continues with military leaders and soldiers who crowned themselves seigniors of the city for short periods, but who caused serious damage: Francesco Sforza, Antonio Colonna, Niccolò Fortebracci and his son Carlo, and in conclusion Niccolò Piccinino, who gained power after a siege which lasted several days. From then onwards, Assisi entered the sphere of influence of the Papal States once and for all, so much so that in 1542 Giovani Andrea Cruciani, the governor elected by Pope Paul III, issued a decree which abolished the 'bipolarism' of the city, divided into an upper and a lower part, and into the Guelphs and the Ghibellines, in order not only to restore peace, but above all to take away the local electoral system from divisions between the two rival factions, imposing new and controllable ways dictated by Rome.

In conclusion, St. Francis's presence was of major importance in the history of the city. He was born here in 1182, the son of a merchant, Pietro di Bernardone. After the restless years of his youth he changed his lifestyle completely, imitating the life of Christ and following the ideals of the Gospels: poverty, chastity and seclusion from the world. Having gathered together a small group of 'brothers', he started preaching and obtained the acknowledgement and approval of his newly formed Order by Pope Honorius III. His example was also followed by Santa Chiara, and by other young women who later on founded the Franciscan Second Order (Second'Ordine). After an intense period of preaching reaching out even to the East, Francis retired to Mount Verna where he received the stigmata. He died sickly, and almost totally blind in Assisi in 1226.

Almost all the religious buildings in Assisi have some connection with the Saint: the imposing Basilica on two levels was dedicated to him. In the lower part (designed by the architect Ugo Tarchi between 1926 and 1932) houses the Saint's tomb, while in the upper part, elegant in its Gothic shapes with Romanesque influences, there is the famous series of frescoes by Giotto and his school which fortunately survived the earthquake of 1997 which destroyed part of the vault. A church dedicated to Santa Chiara was built next to the perimeter walls and recognizable from the large 14th century arches. Nearby stands the Cathedral of San Rufino, where both Francis and Chiara were baptized. The imposing Rocca Maggiore overlooks the city, destroyed and reconstructed by Cardinal Albornoz, as mentioned above, when in the mid-1300s he regained control over the

Papal Lands in the name of the Pope in Avignon. The grandiose basilica of Santa Maria degli Angeli contains the 'Porziuncola', the small chapel where St Francis used to pray.

Today Assisi is a very lively city, with flourishing tourism, not solely religious. Also, it has many arts and crafts workshops (making articles in iron and wood) and industry, especially in the food sector.

Città di Castello

Situated on the left bank of the Tiber, the Italic town of Città di Castello had little contact with the Etruscans. But, since its foundation having a favourable geographical location, took advantage of the road network, south-western and north-eastern, going as far as central Europe. As a Roman federate *municipium,* under the name *Tifernum Tiberinum* it saw a remarkable development, which was not halted by the arrival of the Lombards, and even the conquest by the Franks was not that traumatic. The Consuls, who were the leaders of the new institutional government (the Commune) were firstly mentioned in the mid-1100s and from then on the history of the Commune of Tiferno could be defined as a story of political intrigue with relations, often difficult, with powerful cities with expansionist aims. On the one hand there were the Papal States and the Empire with the bellicose presence of Frederick II, and on the other hand there were Perugia with Braccio da Montone, Arezzo with the Tarlati family, and Florence with the Medici. In different ways and in different periods, all of these powers tried to dominate the Commune that between the 1200s and the 1400s increased both economically and politically. It developed also thanks to traumatic situations, such as the seigniory of Braccio Fortebracci, the military leader from Montone who ruled over Perugia for a while, and dominated Città di Castello from 1422 to 1424, year of his death. It was the Vitelli family, from Città di Castello, that unravelled to a certain extent the confused situation. They had become wealthy as merchants and began to appear on the political scene from the middle of the 1200s. But only with Nicolò Vitelli can we talk of a true seigniory created not without difficulty and administered by the family. In fact, after having defended Città di Castello in 1474 from the papal siege, Nicolò was exiled from the town by Sixtus IV, and fled to Urbino to the court of the Montefeltro family, who helped him especially from the military point of view, when he tried to re-gain his powerful position, supported also by the Medici. Nicolò's efforts were crowned with success, and from then on he was called 'father of the homeland', and reinforced the position of his family, which was politically very influential. Later his sons Paolo and Vitellozzo succeeded him. This latter was killed in the sadly famous 'Convegno di Senigallia' (Meeting at Senigallia) organized in 1502 by Cesare Borgia in order to rid himself of his alleged enemies. But shortly afterwards the death of Pope Borgia ended the expansionist aims of his son, and the election of Julius II re-established the Papal control over these areas, and restored order and stability in the town, with the re-election of the abolished magistracies, or the Priori (who had their seat in the Communal Palazzo or Palazzo dei Priori, still existing). The Vitelli family continued to take an important role in the town with some important figures like Alessandro, natural son of Paolo, captain at the service of the Medici family and later of the Pope, but also a military architect. He was an eclectic and versatile character whose misfortune was to marry a vile woman, Angela Rossi di San Secondo, already wife of his cousin Vitello. This woman left behind a bad reputation of herself together with her son Vitellozzo.

The publication of the city statutes (1538) dates to the seigniory of the Vitelli family. This collection of laws, which ruled the city life, dates to the 14th century, but in the 1500s these were published in a detailed and precise manner.

After the fall of the Vitelli family dynasty, with hostility and division, the history of the town entered a subdued period that was similar to the other provinces of the Papal States. This town saw a reawakening at the end of the 1700s thanks to the French presence, in the Napoleonic period, later during the rebellions and turmoil of the wars for the Italian Unification, and finally in the period of the annexation to the Kingdom of Italy.

The Vitelli family links its name to charming town palazzi, and to the memory of a court similar to that of Urbino which counted the most important artists and intellectuals of the Italian Renaissance. Worthy of mention are Palazzo Vitelli near Porta Sant'Egidio built in the 1550s together with its garden (today a public garden) and the Palazzina (perfectly restored); and Palazzo Vitelli alla Cannoniera (seat of the Town Art Gallery) built by Alessandro Vitelli for the occasion of his marriage to Angela Rossi di San Secondo (1521-1545) and embellished by the 'well-balanced graffito façade' made by Cristoforo Gherardi who based his work on the preliminary design by Vasari with whom he collaborated. Worthy of inclusion in this brief list is also Palazzo Tommasini (ex Bourbon del Monte) seat of the workshop 'Tela Umbra', founded in 1908 with a philanthropic aim, and of a Museum-Collection of ancient Umbrian textiles. Furthermore there are the churches of the Mendicant orders (St Francis and St Dominic) which are situated next to the cathedral, dedicated to the town patron saint, San Florido, who energetically took part in the reconstruction of the town after the destruction by the Gothic King, Totila.

For several years a horse fair, important for the sector and for the town, has been taking place in the town. While as to manufacturing, mention can be made of the textile industry, reproduction of antique furniture, not forgetting the flourishing typographic sector which is characteristic of this area thanks to the presence of several factories that produce high quality goods, attracting customers, both from the region and outside.

Deruta
by Stefania Zucchini

An internationally renown centre for pottery production, Deruta stands on a hill about fifteen kilometres to the south of Perugia. Documentary sources referring to its foundation, and the early centuries of the town's life, are scant. A local tradition, which is now accepted also by historiography, relates that the town was founded by the inhabitants of Perugia who were escaping from their own city, which Augustus plundered and burned during the *Bellum Perusium* (41-40 BC). The town was named after this event, which can be derived from the Latin verb *diruo* (to destroy). Another tradition recounts that the name of the town comes from the Latin verb *eruo* (to take out). Here, the reference was to the clay quarries which, since Antiquity, have been used for making terracotta. In the modern period, the inhabitants of Deruta (*Derutesi*) used to link the name of their town to a locally-found plant, *ruta* (rue, or "herb of grace"), which still features in the town's coat of arms, above a battlemented tower, and alongside an enormous crowned griffin (the symbol of Perugia). It is a fact that both the art of pottery, documented from the middle of the 13th century, and relations with the ruling Perugia played a fundamental role in the history of Deruta in the Middle Ages and in the modern period. The first document bearing a reference to Deruta dates to 1186. This is a certificate issued by the chancellery of Henry VI for the Commune of Perugia, in which the Emperor granted the inhabitants of Perugia jurisdiction over the whole *contado* (the extended area beyond the city itself), but with some exceptions, such as the properties of the *nobiles de Diruta* (noble families of Deruta). Thus, at the end of the 12th century, Deruta was still a self-governing town, presumably ruled by a local aristocracy closely connected to the Emperor. In the 13th century, the inhabitants of Deruta established a Commune, led by a *Consul* or a *Dominus* (a title that makes us think of the rule of the aristocracy), even though in this period Perugia was playing the role of ruler. In this period, Deruta issued its own statute, which was recognized by Perugia, and which still exists today, in a later copy from 1465. From this and other sources (such as land registers) we learn that, for a long period of time, Deruta's economy was based on agriculture (on the plain) and on arts and crafts (on the hill, especially in the town centre). The Tiber runs through the plain, which is thus very fertile, and it was characterized, as well as by a series of small properties, by large estates owned generally by important religious bodies from Perugia, such as the Casalina estate, which was the major property of the Benedictine monastery of San Pietro, and which today is owned by the Perugia Foundation for Agrarian Education. But arts and crafts themselves, especially pottery production, represented the most important business of the inhabitants of Deruta. There are still many different signs of its importance. First, the fact that there was a remarkable demand for products from Deruta. Suffice it to say that, between the 13th and the 14th centuries, the parish church of San Niccolò in Deruta, which came under the authority of the Capitol of the Cathedral of Perugia, paid its annual taxes neither in money nor in agricultural products but in pottery, two baskets, and one sack of pottery. From the early 1300s, Deruta was handed the privilege of supplying earthenware and tableware to the Fransciscan monastery in Assisi. In 1550, at the height of the Renaissance, the geographer Leandro Alberti, describing Deruta, lauded the quality and characteristics of the local majolica ware, which was so refined that it achieved fame throughout Italy. In the following century, despite the general economic crisis of the Papal States, Deruta's pottery continued to be highly valued. Even in the periods in which production decreased, and quality declined, local artisans distinguished themselves for their creative and organizational skills, besides their awareness of being part of an important tradition. A clear example of this is the assembly of 1528, where 28 pottery-makers from Deruta met to discuss the crisis in the sector, due also to the epidemic at the time, and the devastating march of Charles V's troops on their way back from the plunder of Rome. They worked out a detailed "restyling" plan, starting with retraining of the workforce. From an institutional point of view, from 1540 (the year of the Salt War, which determined the definitive subjection to Perugia and the Pope) onwards, and up until 1860, Deruta was ruled by the papal government. There are only two short interruptions, in which the town was first annexed to the Roman Republic (1798-1800) and later to the Napoleonic Empire (1809-1814).

Deruta was also well-known in the production of ceramics that connected with the traditional Renaissance production, represented by the 'piatti da pompa' (large dishes for special occasions or included as part of bridal dowries), 'piatti a quartieri' (with borders divided into sectors with different motifs), 'albarelli' (vases for chemist's shops) and with the 'coppe amatorie' (displaying in its centre the figure of a woman or a 'putto'). Important examples of these kinds of ceramics are now in the Regional Museum of Ceramics, which is housed in the former monastery of St. Francis in the town centre of Deruta). This Museum is arranged on three levels: on the ground floor, besides the various exhibition areas, a special room is dedicated to the history of ceramics. Here the protagonist are the archaic ceramics from the 1300s, displaying their characteristic two-coloured decoration (dark brown and green) with three different kinds of motif: leaves, knots and anthropomorphic figures. Furthermore, the history of the development of this art, as regards production, techniques, styles and patron-customers from the Renaissance to the 1900s, is displayed on the upper floors, where there are not only extraordinary examples of ceramics decorated with the 'lustre' technique (metallic iridescence), but also tableware (jugs, cake stands, dishes and earthenware etc.) and products for daily use from the Renaissance to the present day.

Gubbio

Gubbio was founded by the Umbri, and preserves one of the most important and famous epigraphic remains from the period prior to that of the Romans, the 'Tavole

Eugubine', dating to the 3rd-1st century BC. They are seven bronze panels of different sizes which are inscribed in the language of the Umbri, partly Umbrian letters and partly Latin letters, describing the rituals of the Grabovia triad (Jove, Mars and Vofione), which are interestingly informative for the town.

The fact that Gubbio became a Roman *municipium* favoured its social and economic development, as testified to by important remains such as the theatre of the 1st century AD, which is still used for summer performances. During the Gothic war, Gubbio was violently destroyed by Totila as happened to other places in the region. It was immediately rebuilt by the Byzantines and, after the construction of imposing towers, was included in a system of fortresses which had to defend the Via Flaminia. Unfortunately this system did not prevent the town from being occupied by the Lombards. After the fall of the Lombards and the beginning of the domination by the Franks, Gubbio remained for a long period of time in that group of towns included in the Carolingian donation. After which, its history was characterized by the presence of important families that, thanks to their castles, dominated the environs, and later arrived in the town in order to dominate the newly born Commune. These families were: the Bosoni Raffaelli, Gabrielli, both branches of Frontone and Cantiano, the aristocratic family of Biscina, and of the Della Branca. The Guelph Cante and Bino Gabrielli stood out, and thanks also to the favour of the Roman Curia ruled the town and took possession of the archbishopric. The attempts of the Ghibellines to achieve power were unsuccessful, and for decades the Gabrielli became the seigniors of Gubbio. But their political and territorial aims collided with those of the powerful Perugia and with the expansionism of the Papal States and of the Montefeltro family. Relations between Perugia and Gubbio were characterised by continuous conflicts, which saw victories (that of Gubbio in 1151, attributed to the intervention of St Ubaldo) and defeats on both sides up until the peace treaty of 1273 under which the dominant part was obliged to return the areas previously occupied to the Commune of Gubbio. The Pope in Avignon intervened sending Cardinal Egidio Albornoz to Italy. His task was to restore the dominance of the Papal States over this area, thus he besieged and occupied the town in 1354 bringing it again under the Pope's rule, but for a short period of time. Shortly afterwards, the Gabrielli family was the protagonist of clamorous events that led to remarkable consequences: the powerful bishop Gabriello Gabrielli, who was an influential personality and seignior of the town, in order to counter the expansionist pressure of the Duke of

Urbino, decided to hand over the town to Prince Charles the Short who was passing through central Italy to go to the Kingdom of Naples to fight against Queen Joan I. Gabrielli's death and the complete indifference of the prince opened Gubbio's doors to Antonio da Montefeltro, who dominated the town from 1384 to 1404, guaranteeing a period of relative peace and prosperity. This favourable climate also continued under Antonio's successors, both from the house of Montefeltro and from that of the Della Rovere, due to the extinction of the former family. In fact, in 1508 as Guidubaldo I did not have heirs, he nominated his successor Francesco Maria I, son of Giovanni della Rovere and of Giovanna da Montefeltro. He married Eleonora Gonzaga, who was well considered in all the courts thanks to her intellect and morality, and thus he opened the door to a prestigious future for his lineage. Their son Guidubaldo II married first of all Giulia Varano, heir to the Duchy of Camerino, and after Vittoria Farnese niece of Pope Paul III, who was trustee of the Della Rovere patrimony. In 1624, their son Francesco Maria II agreed and had the statute of the town published by the printer Marco Antonio Triangolo. The Duke himself, who had pushed for the marriage between his niece Vittoria and the Grand Duke of Tuscany, Ferdinando II, let the Duchy fall under the rule of the Papal States after his death. Excepting for the brief periods of French government, Gubbio was part of the Papal States up until 1860, during which time it declined on all fronts.

Imposing and important monuments of Gubbio's communal period are still visible, such as Palazzo dei Consoli, one of the most beautiful communal palazzi of all of Italy, with its monumental entrance door and the elegant two-lancet and ogival windows, and the 13th century Palazzo del Capitano del Popolo with its particular curved façade. Furthermore there is the Ducal Palazzo commissioned by Federico da Montefeltro and built on top of the former communal buildings of which a large vault is still visible. This palazzo is characterized by the large entrance door and by the palatial courtyard perfectly proportioned. Last but not least, a basilica situated on Mount Ingino is dedicated to the town's Patron Saint, Sant'Ubaldo. This is linked to the town by a cable car.

Gubbio is also well-known for its ceramics, which boast a tradition dating to the Renaissance and saw a wide distribution between the end of the 15th century and the middle of the 16th century, also thanks to the presence of an important master, Mastro Giorgio, who here had his workshop.

Spoleto

The town of Spoleto boasts an important history. Originally inhabited by the Umbri, it is situated on a dominating hill overlooking the Valle Umbra, and has a well fortified perimeter wall. From the 3rd century BC, as a Roman colony on the Via Flaminia it saw a lengthy period of growth under the shadow of Rome. The theatre and the extraordinary Druso Arch bears witness to this prosperous past. Even in the difficult period of the Barbaric invasions, Spoleto was spared by Theodoric, farsighted king of the Ostrogoths, but not by Totila, king of the Goths, who destroyed it during the Gothic war. It was occupied and destroyed as other Umbrian cities. Narses, general of Justinian, who came to Italy to fight and defeat the Goths, which he did, undertook the rebuilding the town and especially its walls. But the real turning point in the history of Spoleto came about when it was conquered by the Lombards, who, after an initial period of destruction, started the establishment of Duchies, administered by Dukes, who had the power of public officials. These Dukes settled in the important cities situated on the important roads. The Duchy of Spoleto was no different with its capital in the city. In its period of maximum expansion, the Duchy included the Piceno areas (Ascoli, Fermo, and Potenza Picena), the Valeria area (Norcia and Rieti, only to mention the most important cities) and the Tuscia area (Spoleto, Spello, Assisi and Terni), reaching the border of another Lombard Duchy, the Duchy of Benevento.

The defeat of the Lombards by the Franks changed the political order, if not the territorial organization, turning the Dukes into representatives of the regal central power also close to the Pope who summoned Charlemagne as papal defender, who later was very generous in donating properties to the Church. The Empire continued to consider this area important, but their interest collided with that of the Pope, especially those of Innocent III, who between 12th and 13th century planned the establishment of a Papal State which included: the Duchy of Spoleto, the Campagna and Marittima (to the south of Rome), the Marca di Ancona and the Properties of San Pietro in Tuscia (to the north of Rome going as far as Orvieto).

The Pope's plans for the Duchy, legitimated by the Carolingian donations, came onto a collision course with the presence of an Imperial delegate in those territories, Konrad of Urslingen, who realizing his military limits, and isolation due to the void of power after Henry VI's death, decided his subjection to the Pope, freeing the inhabitants from their loyalty to the Empire. In this way all the major cities of the Duchy, Spoleto as Perugia, acknowledged the rule of the Pope (1198). From that moment the history of the city was that of its territory, of the Duchy, which became one of the Provinces of the Papal States, evermore regimented, centralized and powerful. Each province had its own Chancellor, a lay or secular official with ample administrative powers, had its own Parliament made up of the delegates of the city and the feudatories, and later on it also had its Treasurer, an official elected in Rome in order to administer the finances of the provincial government. An important period in the history of Spoleto and of the Duchy came with the arrival in Italy of the Legate, Cardinal Egidio Albornoz. In the middle of the 1300s, he established the seat of his delegation in this very place, built a Rocca and from here he worked to restore the earlier order. After the return of the Pope to Rome, the end of the schism, and the restoration of the Papal States by Pope Martin V (1424), Spoleto maintained its prestigious position and became seat of the various Governors, amongst whom several from important families. We can mention Lucrezia Borgia, daughter of Pope Alexander VI, who was sent here as governor for a very short period (1499), during which she lived with her court in the Rocca. In the following centuries the history of Spoleto was conditioned by the papal policy of centralization. This lead to an economic decline but fortunately not to a cultural decline, due to the presence in the 1600s of an important Academy, the Accademia degli Ottusi. During the period of French government, Spoleto was included initially in the Clitunno Department and later in the Trasimeno Department, where it became a major city, more important than Perugia itself. Again during the period of the restoration of the papal regime, after the Napoleonic period, the city became the centre of one of the Delegations which had been created copying the organization of the previous French departments. In 1860, Spoleto also entered into the newly born Kingdom of Italy, after voting for the annexation.

It was thanks to Cardinal Albornoz that the Rocca was built (it has been perfectly restored and today is the seat of cultural events relating to the Spoleto Festival). The imposing construction stands on the top of St Elia hill overlooking the valley, the roads and the city itself. The construction began in 1359 and ended in 1370, designed by the military architect Matteo Gattaponi. Nearby the bridge of the Torri, which was finished by Cardinal Albornoz, using pre-existing structures in order to guarantee a water supply to the Rocca.

The cathedral dedicated to Santa Maria Assunta bears witness to its long history starting from its façade. It was built over the pre-existent church of Santa Maria del Vescovado, has a Romanesque façade with an extraordinary rose window and a mosaic depicting the Redeemer. It was restored at the end of the 1400s, and an elegant arcade overlooking the square was added, and it was at the heart of city life in the medieval commune. Over the years it has become an evocative and exclusive area for cultural activities linked to the Festival, which attracts cultural tourism to the city, interested also in the surrounding areas, both for the presence of numerous castles and the production and sale of high quality olive oil.

Todi

Like Perugia, Todi boasts a dual origin, Etruscan and Umbrian. The Etruscan origin is testified to by the remains of the Necropolis, and the Umbrian origin by the local dialect. The town was conquered by Rome in the 4th century BC, became a colony and later a *municipium* of relative importance (a theatre, amphitheatre and a section of the travertine walls are still visible today). The effects of the Germanic invasions and of the Gothic War – which were ruinous for the Umbrian cities, especially the invasion by Totila, King of the Goths – did not spare Todi, which saw a progressive reduction of its *contado* without being capable of resistance. In fact, in this period noble families grew in importance and later became very influential in shaping the history of the city. These families were the Arnolfi family, the Baschi, Montemarte, Alviano and the Atti family. Inside the walls we can only hypothesize the presence of a bishop due to the lack of documentation, who would have been the representative of the city for all of the 11th century not only for the religious sector, but also the civil sector. This was an authority 'which has a close relationship with the urban community', even if for a certain period it was in tandem with a lay official, maybe a Count (Rapizzone) of the Arnolfi family. Todi was part of that strategy to recover the Imperial territories carried out decisively by Pope Innocent III, so much so that in 1198 it was included in the list of cities subjected to the Pope, together with Città di Castello, Gubbio and Perugia with their territories. The policy of Pope Innocent III of dividing the territories into districts led to the creation of several provinces: Campagna and Marittima, Duchy of Spoleto, Marca di Ancona and Patrimony of San Pietro in Tuscia, though was of little significance to Todi as it was unwilling to accept being part of a province. In the middle of the 12th century, a group of Todi inhabitants gathered around the leading figure of a bishop in order to govern the city, and this led to the establishment of a Commune as an independent government administered initially by Consuls and later by a Podestà (from 1201) and a Capitano del Popolo. During the Communal period Todi had a remarkably florid economy and was politically stable, this had at its base a solid system of alliances with the powerful Perugia, an alliance with Terni and Amelia which allowed its territorial expansion to the south, and a series of acts of subjection agreed with the powerful families of the *contado* (especially with the Alviano family). Furthermore these agreements assured the city the jurisdiction and the financial income from an ever larger territory which reached as far as the rival Orvieto which was under its control, and last but not least a decisive support of papal policy and support from the Pope. The idea that Todi was Ghibelline is not correct as in actual fact it was Guelph but with a unique Guelph policy: it was loyal to the Papal States but against any inclusion into a province as was Innocent III's plan. Thus it supported and defended its self-government from the provincial system. Eventually its self-government was acknowledged by Pope Boniface VIII, the Pope who had a special relationship with Todi, where he had spent his youth with his uncle, Pietro Caetani, town bishop from 1252 to 1276. Besides Pietro Caetani, the bishop had always played an important role as he guaranteed 'a well-balanced government based on a fair partition of power between the two city factions', the Guelphs and Ghibellines. Furthermore the city had the patronage of some important personalities, such as Cardinal Matteo d'Acquasparta, Cardinal Matteo Rosso Orsini and the Bentivenga family. The lure of Rome explains also the influence it had in the election of the Podestà who came from the major baronial families (Savelli,

Orsini and Caetani). The cohesion within the influential class of the city – which was strictly linked and often related to the abovementioned figures – explains the fact that it was slow in reforming institutionally the commoners gathered into Guilds and in the establishment of the office of the Capitano del Popolo. Even the great town planning developments, which in other towns had come with popular governments as had happened in Perugia, in Todi these building works came under the rule of a Podestà and were backed by Boniface VIII. This was the case of the building works in the square, the construction of the communal palazzi, and the building of the church and the monument of San Fortunate. This latter in particular, which holds the corpse of the Patron Saint, is also the church of the Franciscans, who were much more numerous than the Dominicans and the Agostinians, while the Servi di Maria settled in the quarter of Borgo Nuovo, whose inhabitants for the most part were artisans. The 1200s are also the century of Jacopone, who was born in Todi (1230-1306) and who later entered the Franciscan Order. He became a strong supporter of the strict spiritual life, and consequently via his lauds he accused the clergy and the Pope of corruption. Thus Jacopone was a son of Todi but he was alien to his birthplace, because he was in continuous conflict with the clergy (first of all Boniface VIII) who were the supporters of the city government. 'The principle friends of Todi are Jacopone's enemies'.

The objective of Cardinal Egidio Albornoz, who was sent to Italy by the Pope in Avignon in order to restore order in the papal territories, also touched Todi which, definitively subject to papal rule, was governed by men more or less loyal to the Papal States: the Malatesta family from Rimini, Braccio da Montone, and Francesco Sforza, Duke of Milan. The inevitable decline linked to the papal government was interrupted by that outstanding figure of Bishop Angelo Cesi (1566-1606), who was the patron for several important architectural works and social activities. After him, after the prosperous period of the Accademia degli Stabili, and the French government at the end of the 1700s (Todi was chosen as capital city in the Trasimeno Department), after the period of the Italian Unification, in 1860 the city was annexed to the newly born State of Italy, as were many Umbrian cities.

Palazzo del Podestà and Palazzo del Capitano del Popolo, slightly behind the former, overlook the beautiful square which is completed by Palazzo dei Priori to the southern side and by the Cathedral in front of it, whose construction dates to the 12th and 16th centuries. Nearby there is the church of San Fortunato, larger than the cathedral, whose construction began in 1292 and whose façade is still unfinished. Here the corpse of Jacopone was transferred by bishop Cesi in 1596.

Todi is well-known for the production of wooden antique furniture, but is also famous for an antique market which attracts both Italian and foreign professionals, tourists and connoisseurs.

BIBLIOGRAPHY

L. Andreani, *Todi al tempo di Iacopone*, in *Iacopone da Todi*, Official Records of the International Convention of History (Todi, October 8-11 2000), Spoleto, CISAM, 2002, pp. 21-45.

Assisi, ed. F. Santucci, in *Storia illustrata delle città dell'Umbria*, 6, Milan, Elio Sellino Editore, 1997.

F. Bartoccini, *Perugia tra vecchio e nuovo regime*, in *Storia illustrata delle città dell'Umbria*, 2, Milan, Elio Sellino Editore, 1993, pp. 657-670.

A. Bartoli Langeli, *Le origini del Comune. I Consoli*, in *Storia illustrata delle città dell'Umbria*, 1, Milan, Elio Sellino Editore, 1993, pp. 113-128.

A. Bartoli Langeli – L. Zurli, *L'iscrizione in versi della Fontana Maggiore di Perugia*, Rome, Herder, 1996.

G. Casagrande, *Movimenti religiosi e eresie*, in *Storia illustrata delle città dell'Umbria*, 1, Milan, Elio Sellino Editore, 1993, pp. 257-270.

F. Chiapparino – R. Covino, *La fabbrica di Perugia. Perugia 1907-2007*, Perugia, ICSIM – Comune di Perugia, 2008.

R. Chiacchella, *Perugia nello Stato pontificio,* in *Storia illustrata delle città dell'Umbria*, 2, Milan, Elio Sellino Editore, 1993, pp. 369-384.

R. Covino, *Dall'antifascismo alla Resistenza,* in *Storia illustrata delle città dell'Umbria*, 3, Milan, Elio Sellino Editore, 1993, pp. 817-832.

R. Covino, *L'egemonia moderata e le consorterie,* in *Storia illustrata delle città dell'Umbria*, 2, Milan, Elio Sellino Editore, 1993, pp. 673-688.

E. Curti, *La città romana*, in *Storia illustrata delle città dell'Umbria*, 1, Milan, Elio Sellino Editore, 1993, pp. 81-95.

S. De Cenzo, *La centralità mancata. La questione ferroviaria in Umbria (1845-1927)*, Perugia, CRACE, 2004.

M. Della Porta, *Simboli delle porte*, in *Carte che ridono*, Perugia, Editoriale Umbra, 1987, pp.62-69.

Ducato (Il) di Spoleto, Official Records of the 9th International Convention of the Study of the Early Middle Ages (Spoleto, September 27 - October 2, 1982), Spoleto, CISAM, 1983.

M.C. Fagotti, *Perugia capoluogo della Provincia dell'Umbria*, in *Storia illustrata delle città dell'Umbria*, 2, Milan, Elio Sellino Editore, 1993, pp. 641-656.

A.E. Feruglio, *Perugia etrusca in età arcaica*, in *Storia illustrata delle città dell'Umbria*, 1, Milan, Elio Sellino Editore, 1993, pp. 33-48.

A.E. Feruglio, *La città e il territorio in età ellenistica*, in *Storia illustrata delle città dell'Umbria*, 1, Milan, Elio Sellino Editore, 1993, pp. 49-64.

M.G. Fioriti, *La Rocca Paolina*, in *Storia illustrata delle città dell'Umbria*, 2, Milan, Elio Sellino Editore, 1993, pp. 353-368.

G.B. Furiozzi, *Perugia nel Risorgimento*, in *Storia illustrata delle città dell'Umbria*, 2, Milan, Elio Sellino Editore, 1993, pp. 593-608.

G. Gallo, *La Perugina*, in *Storia illustrata delle città dell'Umbria*, 3, Milan, Elio Sellino Editore, 1993, pp. 769-784.

A. Grohmann, *Perugia*, Roma-Bari, Laterza, 1981 (*Le città nella storia d'Italia*).

G. Gubitosi, *Perugia tra le due Guerre*, in *Storia illustrata delle città dell'Umbria*, 3, Milan, Elio Sellino Editore, 1993, pp. 801-814.

E. Irace, *Le Accademie e la vita culturale*, in *Storia illustrata delle città dell'Umbria*, 2, Milan, Elio Sellino Editore, 1993, pp. 481-496.

E. Irace, *Le Arti e i loro libri in età moderna (secoli XVI-XIX)*, in *"Per buono stato de la citade". Le Matricole delle Arti di Perugia*, catalogue of the exhibition (Perugia, June 20 - September 15, 2001), ed. M. Roncetti, Perugia, Volumnia, 2001, pp. 33-37.

J.-C. Maire Vigueur, *Comuni e signorie in Umbria, Marche e Lazio*, Tourin, Utet, 1987.

J.-C. Maire Vigueur, *Il Comune Popolare*, in *Società e istituzioni dell'Italia comunale: l'esempio di Perugia (secoli XII-XIV)*, I, Perugia, Deputazione di Storia Patria per l'Umbria, 1988, pp. 41-56.

Maestri, insegnamenti e libri a Perugia. Contributi per la storia dell'Università (1308-2008), catalogue of the exhibition (Perugia, January-March 2009), ed. C. Frova - F. Treggiari - M.A. Panzanelli Fratoni, Perugia-Milan, University-Skira, 2009.

P. Melograni, *Perugia nella prima Guerra Mondiale*, in *Storia illustrata delle città dell'Umbria*, 3, Milan, Elio Sellino Editore, 1993, pp. 785-800.

E. Menestò, *Omaggio a Todi: la città tra alto e bassomedioevo*, in *Spazi, tempi, misure e percorsi nell'Europa del bassomedioevo*, Official Records of the 22th International Convention of History (Todi, October 8-11, 1995), Spoleto, CISAM, 1996, pp. 1-41.

C. Minciotti Tsoukas, *Dalla conquista francese alla restaurazione*, in *Storia illustrata delle città dell'Umbria*, 2, Milan, Elio Sellino Editore, 1993, pp. 577-590.

M.T. Mori, *Salotti. La sociabilità delle élite nell'Italia dell'Ottocento*, Rome, Carocci, 1998.

M.G. Nico, *Corporazioni e società comunale*, in *"Per buono stato de la citade". Le Matricole delle Arti di Perugia*, catalogue of the exhibition

(Perugia, June 20 - September 15, 2001), ed. M. Roncetti, Perugia, Volumnia, 2001, pp. 19-25.

M.G. Nico - C. Regni, *Il Palazzo come sede del governo comunale*, in *Il Palazzo dei Priori di Perugia*, ed. F.F. Mancini, Perugia, Quattroemme, 1997, pp. 133-151.

U. Nicolini, *Mura della città e mura dei borghi: la coscienza urbanistica di Perugia medievale*, in *Mura e torri di Perugia*, ed. F. Roncalli di Montorio - U. Nicolini - F.I. Nucciarelli, Rome, Istituto Italiano dei Castelli, 1989, pp. 49-77.

U. Nicolini, *Il periodo consolare e podestarile*, in *Società e istituzioni dell'Italia comunale: l'esempio di Perugia (secoli XII-XIV)*, II, Perugia, Deputazione di Storia Patria per l'Umbria, 1988, pp. 25-39.

Perugia, a cura di M. Montella, Perugia, Electa-Editori Umbri Associati, 1993.

Perugina. Cento anni di arte del gusto, Cinisello Balsamo (Milan), Silvana Editoriale, 2007.

C. Regni, *Da Braccio da Montone ai Baglioni*, in *Storia illustrata delle città dell'Umbria*, 1, Milan, Elio Sellino Editore, 1993, pp. 273-286.

G. Riganelli, *Perugia nell'alto medioevo*, in *Storia illustrata delle città dell'Umbria*, 1, Milan, Elio Sellino Editore, 1993, pp. 97-112.

R. Rossi, *La liberazione e la ripresa demografica*, in *Storia illustrata delle città dell'Umbria*, 3, Milan, Elio Sellino Editore, 1993, pp. 849-864.

S. Sacchi, *Dalla crisi della mezzadria al Piano regionale*, in *Storia illustrata delle città dell'Umbria*, 3, Milan, Elio Sellino Editore, 1993, pp. 881-895.

M.R. Silvestrelli, *L'edilizia pubblica del Comune di Perugia: dal "Palatium Comunis" al "Palatium Novum Populi"*, in *Società e istituzioni dell'Italia comunale: l'esempio di Perugia (secoli XII-XIV)*,

II, Perugia, Deputazione di Storia Patria per l'Umbria, 1988, pp. 482-604.

M.R. Silvestrelli, *La città medievale. Edifici, vie, piazze*, in *Storia illustrata delle città dell'Umbria*, 1, Milan, Elio Sellino Editore, 1993, pp. 145-156.

S. Sottani, *Le origini dell'Università. Bartolo e Baldo*, in *Storia illustrata delle città dell'Umbria*, 1, Milan, Elio Sellino Editore, 1993, pp. 209-220.

Statuto del Comune di Perugia del 1279, I, *Testo*, ed. S. Caprioli with the collaboration of A. Bartoli Langeli, C. Cardinali, A. Maiarelli, S. Merli; II, *Descrizioni e indici*, ed. A. Bartoli Angeli, Perugia, Deputazione di Storia Patria per l'Umbria, 1996.

Statuto del Comune e del Popolo di Perugia del 1342 in volgare, a cura di M.S. Elsheikh, 3 voll., Perugia, Deputazione di Storia Patria per l'Umbria, 2000.

Umbria. Natura, arte, storia, tradizione e civiltà di una regione unica al mondo, Città di Castello-Firenze, Provincia di Perugia, 2000.

S. Zucchini, *Università e dottori nell'economia del comune di Perugia. I registri dei "Conservatori della Moneta" (secoli XIV-XV)*, Perugia, University of Perugia – Deputazione di Storia Patria per l'Umbria, 2008.

D. Waley, *I Comuni delle Terre della Chiesa da Innocenzo III all'Albornoz*, in *Società e istituzioni dell'Italia comunale: l'esempio di Perugia (secoli XII-XIV)*, I, Perugia, Deputazione di Storia Patria per l'Umbria, 1988, pp. 137-153.

Printed in February 2010
by Industrie Grafiche Pacini Editore S.p.A.
Via A. Gherardesca • 56121 Ospedaletto • Pisa • Italy
Tel. +39 050 313011 • Fax +39 050 3130300
Internet: http://www.pacinieditore.it